GETTING READY TO TEACH THIRD GRADE

Written by Glenda Frasier

Photos by Bruce Hazelton

Illustrated by Cary Pillo

Rosalie Cochran

Louisa Tennille

We warmly thank the community of the Fern Avenue School of Torrance, California, especially Mrs. Rosalie Cochran, principal; Ms. Louisa Tennille, third-grade teacher; and students, parents, and caregivers of Ms. Tennille's third-grade class.

Project Manager: Barbara G. Hoffman

Editor: Karibeth Soto

Book Design: Anthony D. Paular

Cover Design: Anthony D. Paular

Pre-Press Production: Daniel Willits

FS122005 Getting Ready to Teach Third Grade
All rights reserved—Printed in the U.S.A.
23740 Hawthorne Blvd.
Torrance, CA 90505

Let us put our minds together and see what life we can make for our children.

—Tatanba Iotanko (Sitting Bull) 1877

CHAPTER ONE: INTRODUCTIONS

When I began writing this book, I discovered I was sharing all the things I wish I had known 29 years ago as I entered the third-grade classroom door. After experiencing hundreds of classroom joys and challenges and raising two boys through those third-grade years, I have a better grasp of what is critically important, where one has some latitude, and what things change through the year.

I hope using this book gives you a step ahead in your first year of teaching third-grade. Use it to make planning easier. Use it as a guide to developing workable and simple assessment tools. Use it to help you apply all that theory you've learned to the classroom and to working with your excited and interested students. Have a wonderful year!

THRILLING THIRD GRADERS

If you are thrilled with your world, happy to be with friends, interested in everything, responsible for yourself, and daring . . . you *might* be a third grader.

Third graders are usually eight to nine years old. For a student in third grade, many things are changing. Growth spurts have slowed and the student's motor coordination begins to improve. Playing games that require eye-hand coordination, such as baseball or basketball, becomes easier at this age. Coordination activities such as jumping rope, roller skating, and skiing are also easier. Third graders are ready for games with rules, but they are not always consistent in following those rules.

1

Thinking skills for the successful learner multiply at the third-grade level. The thought processes of the student are becoming more structured and organized. Systematic problem solving begins to emerge and the learner starts to apply rules and generalizations to academic situations. The student's grammar and oral language exhibit an understanding of structure and conventions. Third graders begin to master primary knowledge and move to higher thinking levels. While hands-on work is still vital, the student is able to use textbooks and do increased paperwork.

Self-development occurs as the third-grade student achieves success at these tasks and becomes self-confident about risk-taking in unfamiliar areas. The student then becomes more aware of cause and effect in behavioral situations and develops a stronger sense of right and wrong. An eight or nine-year old can evaluate a moral decision with a sense of conscience. However, rules of behavior are not internalized at this stage, so adult guidance is still required.

School attitudes are positive for most third graders. Their enthusiasm for learning and curiosity about the world is remarkable. Most third graders are eager to accomplish tasks by themselves and desire the recognition they receive from adults for their efforts. Some students already prefer a subject, an activity, or a learning style over others. At the third-grade level, many children develop interest in a hobby that may continue for a lifetime.

In social situations, a student's interaction with his or her peers is critical. Around the time they enter third grade, children begin to define themselves by peer values, with both positive and negative results. Those who have a high level of self-worth act naturally in social settings and exhibit tolerance and flexibility with friends. Peer groups are often made up of students of the same sex and help to increase the students' feeling of belonging. These peer groups are formed more on the basis of interests and events rather than random associations. Exclusion from a desired group is extremely hurtful to a child of this age.

A third grader's emotional bond is strongly tied to his or her family. Children in this age group seek independence by attempting to choose their own activities. Brief separation from their parents becomes more comfortable as slumber parties and peer events become more frequent. Family support is critical for a child's stable emotional development through this period. If support is lacking, the school environment must supplement the child's needs so that a positive self-concept will develop.

TIP!

At the beginning of the year have students complete the Student Information Sheet (page 93). Attach a photo to the form. At the end of the year have students complete a new form, and attach another photo. Compare the two—what a difference!

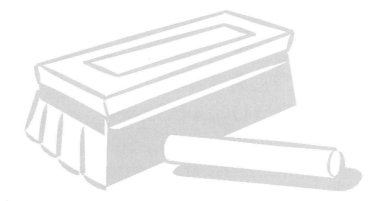

> **Education in the long run is an affair that works itself out between the individual student and his opportunities. Methods of which we talk so much play but a minor part. Offer the opportunities, leave the student to his natural reaction on them, and he will work out his personal destiny, be it a high one or a low one.**
>
> **—William James, speech, <u>Stanford's Ideal Destiny</u>, Stanford University, 1906**

THIRD GRADE CURRICULUM OVERVIEW

This section is presented in alphabetical order by content area. The sequence is Language Arts, Mathematics, Multicultural Education, Physical Education, Science and Health, Social Studies, Technology, and Visual and Performing Arts (which includes Music).

In this overview section you will read about the concepts that are to be addressed in third grade. In Chapter Two—Bringing the Curriculum to Life— you will find in each content area a list of skills generally accepted as appropriate for third grade. After the lists of skills, you will find activities that you can use to teach the skills.

The content and curriculum information presented in this book is provided as a reference. It is not intended to replace your school or district's course of study or curriculum guides. As additional references, you should read the standards published by national teacher organizations such as the National Council of Teachers of Mathematics or the National Council of Teachers of English. Your school or district resource centers will probably have copies of these documents that you can use as references.

Parts of the curriculum sections of this book are based on the Standards of the National Council of the Teachers of Mathematics, the National Council of the Teachers of English, and the National Research Council of the National Academy of Sciences. Other references used are state frameworks and school district curricula from Illinois, California, Nebraska, Massachusetts, Washington, and New York.

Language Arts

Language Arts is a broad area of the curriculum which includes reading, writing, listening, and speaking. Through each of these processes, students express what they know, what they think, and what they value about the world. They make connections between information they know and information they don't know.

Your school or district may have adopted textbooks or other language arts programs that include grammar, spelling, activity, and workbooks, or there may be specific guidelines you are expected to follow. Check with the curriculum coordinator or principal at your school before the school year begins.

Concepts

- Language is used to communicate ideas across time and space.

- Language allows us to express our life experiences in general and with reference to specific ideas and values that we can name. We also use language to better understand and share ourselves with others.

- What we understand and our ability to think about it is shaped by our knowledge, decisions we make, and how we solve problems.

- How we use language shapes events which in turn shape our language. Our English vocabulary grows through the introduction of words from the sciences, war, and rapidly changing technology.

Three components are important to developing the art of language in your classroom. The first is the use of literature, the second is easy access to many books and other educational media, and the third is an emphasis on writing as a process.

Literature

Books create a bridge between the "real world" and your classroom, and between different curricular areas. Good literature can make any information interesting and accessible.

Library Media Resources

Your students should have regular access to a variety of materials from which they can select according to their own interests. You will need to develop a classroom library as well as use the resources of the school and local public libraries.

Writing

The process of speech-to-print is crucial to language development. The writing process includes several stages—prewriting, drafting, receiving responses, revising, editing, and in many cases postwriting. Through the writing process students develop their writing and related skills. They also improve their spoken language through discussion of their work and the work of others.

Processes

Students read and comprehend grade-level material independently, both fiction and non-fiction. They develop their knowledge of common spelling conventions and patterns, and recognize and use conventions of print such as paragraphs and end-sentence punctuations. They make predictions, summarize reading, and answer questions that require analysis, synthesis, and evaluation about grade-level material. They learn to support their answers. Students are expected to formulate questions about what they hear, see, and read. They begin to develop the scientific learning process of hypothesizing (What if...).

Students begin to explore the origins of words, and to use the library media center as a place to develop their information retrieval and communication skills. They continue to analyze root words in vocabulary, adding or changing a word's beginning part or its ending part, and discussing how the changes in the word affect the meaning of the word. Their writing should reflect growing understanding of formal sentence structure, the four basic types of sentences, and how to use the sentences in written paragraphs. Phonetic principles of decoding are used to support correct pronunciation of new words but major emphasis is on learning to explore and use dictionaries, glossaries, and other reference books to learn new words, their pronunciations, and their meanings.

> We become not a melting pot but a beautiful mosaic. Different people, different beliefs, different yearnings, different hopes, different dreams.
>
> —Jimmy Carter, speech, Pittsburgh, Pennsylvania, October 27, 1976

Mathematics

In third grade, students are deepening their knowledge of place value and their understanding of and skill with addition, subtraction, multiplication, and division of whole numbers. They estimate, measure, describe objects in space, and they use patterns to help solve problems. They are beginning to recognize and use abstractions. They begin to develop understanding of fractions and decimals and the relationship between the two.

- "Knowing" mathematics is "doing" mathematics. A person gathers, discovers, or creates knowledge in the course of some purposeful activity.

- Mathematics is a foundation discipline for other disciplines. Mathematical models, structures, and simulations are applicable to many disciplines.

- Mathematics is growing and changing. All students need mathematics to be productive citizens of the 21st-century.

Concepts

- In the numeral for a whole number, a one in each place is worth ten in the place to the right of it.

- Division is the inverse operation of multiplication.

- The fraction m/n represents m pieces, each of which is 1/n.

- Fractions are added or subtracted by expressing them with a common denominator.

- The unit of measurement for areas is the unit square and for volume measurement it is the unit cube.

- Data can be displayed in graphical forms that make it easier to make predictions about related events.

Multicultural Education

Multicultural education is an interdisciplinary subject and the concepts should be part of the context of every lesson you present. The goal is to help students develop positive attitudes about themselves and other cultures. Through an anti-biased curriculum students learn to appreciate, respect, and value differences.

Concepts

- Our identities are shaped and influenced by the families, schools, and communities in which we live. We share a common bond with the people with whom we share our communities.

- Our community is made up of many cultures which have all impacted and influenced it and our economy.

- Each person has dignity and worth. We are interdependent. A sense of community and trust builds unity and harmony. People working cooperatively together can find solutions to problems. Conflict can be managed and resolved through peaceful methods. There is no room for stereotyping, prejudice, and discrimination in our community.

Curricular activities should build the student's intellectual and interpersonal skills, including exhibiting pride in one's own cultural heritage, differentiating between dislikes and prejudice, recognizing different points of view, identifying obvious stereotypes, showing empathy for individuals or groups in difficult situations, and planning ways to create a peaceful school and community environment. Correct terminology should be used to identify various racial and ethnic groups and respect should be shown for all cultures.

Physical Education

In third grade, students are becoming more proficient in locomotor skills, manipulative movements, and group social skills. Most boys and girls become more active in physical fitness and recreational activities.

Concepts

- Different kinds of movements promote the development of different abilities. Locomotor skills are ways to move from one place to another. Nonlocomotor skills such as stretching, swinging, swaying, and shaking promote flexibility. Manipulative skills such as catching, throwing, batting, and dribbling promote eye-hand coordination. Movement involves both small and large muscles. To perfect their motor skills students need repetitive practice. Movement can be coordinated into rhythmic patterns.

- Physical fitness concepts include developing strong arm and shoulder muscles, promoting flexibility, muscular strength and endurance, and cardiorespiratory endurance. We can prevent excessive fatigue by knowing our own limitations.

- Self-image can be improved through physical fitness. Practice and repeated attempts to attain a goal may be necessary to attain that goal. Movement is a medium through which we can express feelings and emotions.

- Social development through physical education includes several important concepts. Majority decisions should be accepted gracefully. Praising and recognizing effort is better than negative criticism. We should always try our best, even if we are losing.

- Participating in recreational activities is fun. Our skills develop and improve through practice.

Science and Health

Science Concepts

Most state science standards or frameworks are based on the National Science Education Standards (NSES). The NSES presents content standards by grade ranges K–4, 5–8, and 9–12. Consequently third-grade science topics vary considerably from state to state, district to district, and school to school. The NSES K–4 content standards published in 1996 follow.

Unifying Concepts and Processes
- Systems, order, and organization
- Evidence, models, and explanation
- Change, constancy, and measurement
- Evolution and equilibrium
- Form and function

Science as Inquiry
- Abilities necessary to do scientific inquiry
- Understandings about scientific inquiry

Physical Science
- Properties of objects and materials
- Position and motion of objects
- Light, heat, electricity, and magnetism

Life Science
- Characteristics of organisms
- Life cycles of organisms
- Organisms and environments

Earth and Space Science
- Properties of earth materials
- Objects in the sky
- Changes in the earth and sky

Science and Technology

- Abilities to distinguish between natural objects and objects made by humans

- Abilities of technological design

- Understanding about science and technology

Science in Personal and Social Perspective

- Personal health

- Characteristics and changes in populations

- Types of resources

- Changes in environments

- Science and technology in local challenges

History and Nature of Science

- Science as a human endeavor

Curriculum Content

Following you will find a sample curriculum that reflects science topics frequently presented in third grade.

Physical Science

- Matter exists as solid, liquid, and gas. It changes state with the addition or loss of heat.

- Matter has weight (mass) and takes up space.

- Objects can be described, sequenced and/or classified in respect to their position, distance, motion, and time of occurrence.

- Energy has several forms and the sun is our primary source of energy.

- Materials can be described and classified according to whether or not they conduct electricity.

- Electricity is an energy source which is used to run machines and provide light and heat.

Life Science

- There is great diversity among living organisms, including microorganisms, which may be classified by similarities and differences.

- The oceans contain an immense variety of living organisms.

- Plants and animals are interdependent and are adapted to their environment by their structure, function, and behavior through time.

- When organisms die, their life functions cease and their bodies decompose.

- All living organisms, including human beings, have special needs and functions.

- An organism obtains what it needs from the environment and is interdependent with many other living organisms.

- Green plants get their energy from the sun.

- Animals get their energy from eating plants and/or animals.

Earth Science

- The motion of objects in space is predictable.

- The moon, earth's natural satellite, is the only body in the solar system that human beings have yet visited.

- The sun, our closest star, is the source of energy for life on earth, and for the water cycle and other weather phenomena.

- Clouds have characteristics by which they can be described and classified.

- Air is a part of the earth's atmosphere; wind is moving air.

- Water is essential for living things to survive; the main sources of fresh water are rain and melted snow.

- Earthquakes occur when parts of the earth move.

- Volcanic eruptions occur when magma (melted rock) is forced through openings in the earth's crust.

- Safety precautions can reduce injury to people and damage to property when disasters occur.

Health

Health is closely allied with science. It can also be an interdisciplinary subject. Many health concepts and skills can be studied as part of your language arts, math, science, and arts programs, and as a separate unit of study.

Every child should have mudpies, grasshoppers, waterbugs, tadpoles, frogs, mud turtles, elderberries, wild strawberries, acorns, chestnuts, trees to climb, animals to pet, hay fields, pinecones, rocks to roll, sand, snakes, huckleberries and hornets—and any child who has been deprived of these has been deprived of the best part of his education.

—Luther Burbank

Concepts

- It's better to be well than ill. Long-term health and well-being requires an investment of time and caring for oneself. A balanced combination of physical activities, rest, recreation, and adequate diet contributes to fitness and cardiovascular health.

- Families take different forms. Each member affects the health of the others. Heredity and environment influence the development of living organisms. Understanding human growth and development through the life cycle leads to an appreciation of oneself and others. The capacity to adjust to, understand, and respect others will enhance one's interpersonal relationships.

- Daily food intake affects our personal health. Food choice is affected by life style, peers, and family economics.

- Making decisions is a process that helps reduce stress and anxiety, helps one gain self-respect, and obtain personal satisfaction. Understanding and liking oneself, making friends, and getting along with others is essential to good mental health. Understanding and coping with emotions in an acceptable way is healthy, while unresolved conflicts cause stress and anxiety which is unhealthy.

- Some substances may be beneficial when used properly, but can disrupt normal body functions when misused. Drugs are substances that change the way the mind and body work. We can be pressured by the environment or by those around us to use substances, but the choice to misuse them remains our own.

- Many factors contribute to diseases and disorders. How much we can control and prevent disease varies.

Social Studies

The goal of a balanced elementary social studies program is to prepare students to participate in society with the knowledge, skills, and civic values that enable them to be actively and constructively involved. Third-grade students explore the geography of their community and use their critical thinking skills to analyze the changes that may have occurred there. Local history is an important part of the curriculum with field trips to the immediate environment to provide important first-hand observations. Students study how people now and long ago met their needs for food, shelter, and clothing.

Social studies is an interdisciplinary subject. Many social studies concepts and skills can be studied as part of your language arts, math, science, and arts programs, as well as a separate unit of study.

Concepts

- People who lived in a locality or community long ago may have met their basic needs differently from people who live in that locale today. The chronological development of a community is called history.

- Each person is worthy of respect and valued as a unique individual.

- The physical characteristics of a place determine how or where a community may develop.

- People who lived in a community long ago left a legacy of local and regional traditions that provides the basis for the cultures of today.

- The scarcity of resources influences the choices that people make in order to meet their needs.

- Every community has a political system which determines how order is established and maintained.

- Individuals are responsible for their own health and for knowing when to seek help from others. The community provides health-care resources. There are many careers in the field of health. A relationship exists between the quality of the environment and human health. We must work together to create and maintain a safe and healthful environment.

- Many accidents can be prevented. Each of us needs to be prepared to act effectively in times of emergency, including life-threatening situations. Identifying and correcting potential hazards and safety can help reduce accidents and save lives.

> We live in a time of such rapid change and growth of knowledge that only he who is in a fundamental sense a scholar—that is, a person who continues to learn and inquire—can hope to keep pace, let alone play the role of guide.
>
> —Nathan M. Pusey, The Age of the Scholar, 1963

Technology

For purposes of this overview, technology is defined as the application of knowledge to manipulate tools, machines, materials, techniques, and technical systems to satisfy human needs and wants.

Technology can be divided into two sections. One is industrial technology which involves learning construction processes and skills using wood, paper, cardboard, and plastic.

The second section is computer technology, which involves learning computer concepts and tools. How schools present this information is changing as fast as computer technology is. States and school districts are developing their academic standards in this field as this book goes to press.

Concepts

- Communication, transportation, and production are components of technology.

- Projects of increased complexity require greater planning and additional assembly or implementation steps.

- Tools and materials cost money. All hand tools are a direct link to simple machines.

- Cooperation, attentiveness, and promptness are as important as job skills in the world of work.

Visual and Performing Arts

Visual Arts

The visual world of the third-grade student expands rapidly. Color and spatial relationships begin to take form, and students develop a conscious regard for realism and detail.

Concepts

- We are surrounded by images and events, natural and human-made, that have visual and tactile qualities. We can describe the world by means of images and symbols with visual and tactile qualities.

- Knowledge of art techniques can help us express and communicate our experiences through art. Originality and personal experience are important to visual expression. Visual arts media can be used to communicate feelings and ideas.

- Art has played an important role in every culture throughout history. Studying art can give us insight into other cultures. We can learn about our creative abilities through art. Clarifying our personal aesthetic values can help us appreciate the aesthetic values of others.

- We can use objective criteria to analyze and interpret art. Using aesthetic values as a basis for making judgments provides informed responses to art and improve personal artwork.

Performing Arts

Most schools and districts require that students have one or more opportunities a year to perform before a large audience. This may take the form of an assembly or a recital. Check with your administrator or new colleagues to find out the requirements at your school.

Music

The third-grade student is at the beginning of continued and coordinated group work. However, activities using individual and pairs of children should still be provided. The student is gaining more control of the voice and of breathing, as the vocal chords and lungs are developing rapidly. The third grader will be interested in musical activities using small muscles, although intricate coordination may be difficult. Students will be interested in how instruments are made and developed. An increasing number of individual differences and abilities will appear.

Concepts

- Rhythm flows on a recurring steady beat. It is divided into sets of accented and unaccented beats. The rhythm of the melody consists of longer and shorter sounds and silences. Meter is the organization of beats into groups of twos or threes.

- A melody is made up of tones with higher or lower pitches, that may change up or down or repeat. When a melody ends on the home tone a feeling of repose is created. Visual symbols can be used to show the relationships between tones. Tones in a melody may go up or down by a step (scale) or skip (chord). A scale is a specific consecutive arrangement of tones.

- The basic form in music is the phrase or musical thought. Identical phrases contribute to the unity of a composition. A song or other composition may have an introduction or a coda. Contrasting phrases provide variety in compositions. Phrases may be partly the same or partly different. A composition with two sections is called a two-part or binary form. A composition with three sections, the last a repeat of the first, is called three-part or ternary form (ABA).

- Songs can be performed with or without accompaniment. Harmony is created when two or more tones are sounded at the same time. Melodies may be combined resulting in a harmonic texture called polyphony (ostinato, countermelody, round, canon). A musical composition may be either major or minor depending on its melody or harmony. A chord consists of three or more tones sounded simultaneously. Harmony may apply to successions of chords. The tonic or I (one) chord creates a feeling of resolution or repose. The dominant or V (five) is an active chord needing resolution when compared to the tonic chord.

- Sound is produced in diverse ways and can be modified. Tempo is relative rather than absolute. Music can move in a fast or slow tempo. Dynamics in music can be louder or softer. Changes of tempo and dynamics provide a source of variety and expressive meaning in a composition. Characteristic qualities of sounds are determined by the types of voices or instruments which produce them (timbre).

- There are sounds (vocal and instrumental) that are expressive of the student's own culture as well as other cultures.

- Music of today can be compared and contrasted with music of the past.

- Musical experience can be used to make intelligent judgments of musical value.

CHAPTER TWO: BRINGING THE CURRICULUM TO LIFE

LESSON PLANNING

Lesson planning is crucial to effectively organize your instruction. Some schools and districts require you to follow the teachers' manuals of commercially prepared textbook series. If your district does not require this, you will be responsible for planning your instructional year. There are as many ways to plan as there are teachers—so there is no one "right" way. The following is a guide.

Planning your program of instruction is like planning a dinner party. Before you begin to plan a dinner party, you know certain things—how many people you have invited and where you're going to hold the party. You have a certain time frame in mind, and you know that you are going to serve dinner.

First you must decide the presentation of your meal: will it be formal or informal; sit-down dinner or buffet? Based on that decision you decide what the menu of your meal will be—a tried-and-true favorite, or something new? Do you want each food course to be completely different, or do you want the meal to have some unifying elements?

When you know the menu, you collect your recipes to review the ingredients and how to put them together. You schedule your purchases and preparation time. Once the dinner is prepared you assess your results by tasting what you prepare, watching people eat the meal, and seeing what is left over.

Long-Term Planning

You can think of lesson planning in the same way as planning the dinner party. You know how many students you have, you know where you are going to teach them, and you know you are going to teach them the content and skills your school or district requires over the the year. You will find this information in your school or district's curriculum guide or course of study. Ask your principal for a copy of the curricular requirements as soon as you can. You know that you need to organize all the information you must teach into a time frame—the school year.

Think about the concepts you want to teach over the next term. Decide what themes (the presentation of your school year) will provide good frameworks for these concepts. (Refer to the Using Themes section on page 17 for examples of themes.) Choose themes that will interest you and your students, that are not too narrow in focus.

Decide what kinds of projects (the menu) will give your students many opportunities to learn and practice their learning. Projects can include anything from reading thirty pages in the textbook to converting your classroom into an imaginary rain forest.

Create, select, or choose activities (*recipes*) that will support the themes and promote the learning and practice of skills (*ingredients*).

Decide how many days or weeks you will need to accomplish your projects. Make a calendar or time-line of the unit.

Now that you know **what** you want to accomplish you need to plan **how** you will accomplish your long-term plans. Your weekly and daily lesson plans are the way to organize your activities (*recipes*) into a feasible schedule.

A lesson-plan book will be a useful purchase if your school or district does not provide one. There are many varieties from which to choose, from the most basic notebook-sized with gridded pages to large plan books that include lesson plan ideas.

Planning Steps

1. Review the curriculum.

2. Develop an overview of your program of instruction for the year— what concepts you will teach when (as a general idea).

3. Choose themes that provide good frameworks for the concepts.

4. Decide what projects will promote the learning you want to see in a classroom within a theme and across the curriculum.

5. Choose activities to develop the skills that you want to focus on during the thematic unit.

6. Develop a calendar or time-line for the unit.

7. Create your weekly and daily plans.

> **We can best understand learning as growth, an expanding of ourselves into the world around us. We can also see that there is no difference between living and learning, that living is learning, that it is impossible, and misleading, and harmful to think of them as being separate.**
>
> **—John Holt, <u>What Do I Do Monday?</u>, 1970**

13

Concepts

Language Arts
- editing and revision process

Mathematics
- explore geometry and the interrelation of division and multiplication

Science

Physical Science - changes in matter

Earth Science - cataclysmic change (earthquakes and volcanoes)

Health
- Drugs are substances that can change us

Social Studies
- Changes of our community (history), current changes, role of geography in change

Theme

Change

Projects

- Explore nets of tetrahedron and cubes.
- Use "Tunka-shila, Grandfather Rock" legend to review the rock cycle - write original "legends" about volcanos and earthquakes.
- Grow crystal gardens - science journal observations
- chocolate chip cookie activities
- topographical map of our area - group project. Survey local wildlife. Why does it live in our neighborhood?
- Make diorama of neighborhood

Skills

(From Bringing the Curriculum to Life section)

- Read and write legends. Keep personal journals. Begin cursive writing (Lang. Arts)
- Make change for $5 and $10 (Math)
- Construct and describe the properties of a cube (Math)
- Estimate and measure length, width, height, surface area, and volume in standard units (Math)
- Develop logical strategies for solving problems (Math)
- Model and construct 3-dimensional forms with a sense of relative proportion and emphasis using clay, bread dough, and other materials. (Vis. Art)
- Acquire relevant factual information and make generalizations about people and events. (Soc. Studies)
- Explore, observe, and organize objects.

Literature Needed

<u>Keepers of the Earth</u> by Michael J. Caduto and Joseph Bruchac (Fulcrum, 1988); <u>The Great Chocolate Chip Cookie Contest</u> by Barbara Douglass (Lothrop, 1985); <u>History of our Town</u> by Smith Brown - local historical society

arrange for visit by Dr. Gray, geologist from the Univ.

Materials Needed

ammonia
salt
bluing
paintbrushes
Flat dish
water containers
charcoal
large sheets of paper

Weekly plans

Make detailed plans and schedule your instruction a week in advance. Include any regular or unusual events in the plan, such as school assemblies, class visitors, library visits, or short school days. Decide what lessons you want to include in the week and fit them into your schedule. The Scheduling section found on page 68 will assist you in deciding when to teach what.

Daily plans

For your daily plans you will want to balance activities that require sitting with activities where your students can move around. To begin the year you should assume that 25 minutes is long enough to require a student to stay focused on the same thing. As they grow, and you get to know them better, you will find what time frame works for your students. You will also discover exactly what a "wide range of abilities" means. You will have some students who can do whatever you ask them to do, well, in less than half the time that other students require. Plan extension activities or extra projects that will engage these students when they have finished required work. In addition, as you are planning, you may want to decide what homework activities to assign.

Planning a lesson

Decide what the focus or purpose of the lesson is. It should be clearly stated, because the clearer your purpose, the easier to design a lesson that accomplishes the purpose. Some examples of purposes follow.

- The purpose of this activity is to have students find many different addends that give the same sum.

- The purpose of this activity is to have students identify the main ideas of their favorite stories.

List the materials that will be needed. If you need to order any supplies or get other items, you can do so in advance.

Plan the introduction to your lesson to give students background knowledge that will help them understand the new information. Literature, songs, and pictures can build background knowledge and motivate your students.

Plan exactly what you are going to do and how you are going to do it. Walk through the procedure in your head. If the lesson involves following directions and/or making something, do the activity yourself before you present it to your class. This will help you identify trouble spots. It is much easier to make necessary adjustments before you present it to a group of excited third graders.

After you present the lesson your students should have time to work independently on the skill you have presented. This gives them the practice necessary to learn it. You may wish to have the students work in small groups.

Planning for Assessment

The final element to consider is how to assess the effectiveness of the lesson. Use informal observations of students involved in the independent activity planned for the lesson combined with formal checks of the work. For more information on record keeping and assessment, see pages 72 through 75.

Thinking through and planning each lesson is essential to your becoming the most effective teacher you can be.

Good teaching is one-fourth preparation and three-fourths theatre.

—Gail Godwin, The Odd Woman, 1974

	Monday	Tuesday	Wednesday	Thursday	Friday
		Special Project – Topographical Map			
8:00	brainstorm project components	discuss local land forms	assign parts of project	continue project	quick check where we are
8:45 Opening					
	Nets Project Exploration				
9:00	take apart cartons, draw nets and other geometric figures		review tetrahedron	explore cubes	explore nets
9:45 Recess	yard duty		yard duty		
	Reading Writing Workshop – continue projects from last week				
		Need to meet with Mary, Pierce, and Alice about capitalization. Review revision process with Maddy, Jonathon, and Tim			
10:00	Guided Reading: Katie, Amanda, Sean, Esther	Guided Reading: Pierce, Tom, Mary, Phoebe	Guided Reading: Pierce, Tom, Mary, Phoebe	Guided Reading: Alex, Esther, Amanda, Susie, Stella	Guided Reading: Katie, Stella, Oscar, Konan, Channon
11:30 Lunch					
12:15	Read to class – The Forgotten Door by Alexander Key				
12:35	Read Legend of Grandfather Rock	Discuss soil components / Dig a hole in garden observe (science journals)	Collect rocks "make" soil	Erosion experiments wind & water	Field trip to Blackberry Farm to meet with Ms. Van Eyck
1:25	PE – basketball passing/game	Art sand painting	PE – basketball passing/game	Art sand painting	
2:15	Music		Music		
3:15 Closing					
3:30 Dismissal					

USING THEMES

Themes are big ideas, larger than facts, concepts, and skills. Using a theme allows you to integrate the various content areas. It will provide you with a framework to guide you in the design and development of your instructional program. A theme can make words and abstract ideas concrete, and help your students see how ideas relate to other ideas and to their own experiences.

Themes link concepts and skills for your students. As you present new lessons framed in the context of your thematic unit, students can easily add the new information to the knowledge they already have. It is easier for students to learn skills, because they have knowledge and experience which create a context within which to apply the skills. Three examples of themes for third grade are Water, Our Community, and Change.

Water

Using the theme of Water, your students could read poetry and literature about bodies of water (language arts), create a terrarium to explore the water cycle, experiment with watercolor (visual arts), write and illustrate books about the local body of water (language arts), explore where the community gets its drinking water (social studies), test the drinking water (science), investigate water as matter in its different forms—solid, liquid, and gas (science), study ocean animals and make stuffed paper sculptures to scale (visual arts and math).

> [It was] an initiation into the love of learning, of learning how to learn, that was revealed to me by my [Boston Latin School] masters as a matter of interdisciplinary cognition—that is, learning to know something by its relation to something else.
>
> —Leonard Bernstein, <u>New York Times</u>, November 22, 1984

Our Community

Using the theme Our Community, your class could explore literature written about your community or ethnic groups that are part of it (language arts), create three-dimensional topographical maps of the area including important land forms (social studies and science), visit local government and public agencies to interview community workers (language arts), visit the local historical society or library to find out about local history (social studies), collect rocks and identify rocks from the area to learn about the prehistoric origins of the area (science), take a survey of the cultural origins of the community (math and social studies), create a mural about the information students discovered (visual arts), and develop a board game about local history (social studies and visual arts).

Change

There is a lot of material that can be used in a thematic unit on Change. This is a very big idea and all aspects of the curriculum can be explored through it. The planning matrix on page 14 shows what can be done with the theme of change. It could be easily expanded to include a life-science component about animals and plants adapting to their environments.

As you get familiar with the curriculum, you will find that your instructional program grows out of it naturally, organizing itself into themes that reflect your interests. The more interested you are in what you are doing, the better you will do it, and the more you will see your kids turn on to learning.

17

LANGUAGE ARTS

As you plan your language arts program, remember that you can use the reading and writing in all curricular areas for assessment purposes. Although language arts processes apply across the curriculum, some specific skills to address are listed below. They are not listed in any particular order.

- Restate and respond appropriately to directions given orally, graphically, in writing, and nonverbally.

- Give directions in several ways for others to complete a certain task. Explain the purpose of the task and what outcomes are expected.

- Create, share, and perform songs, choral verse, poetry, and story theater scripts. Use chanting, rapping, and speech-making techniques appropriately.

- Suggest and imitate vocal phrasing, pitch, dynamics, and intonations appropriate for oral delivery of different kinds of narrated and expository text such as oral reading of lists, labels, and advertisements, cartoon dialogue or drama scripts, sales pitches or simple political speeches.

- Identify and imitate writing styles and illustrations of authors and illustrators named as favorites. Tell why they are favorites.

- Describe personal feelings about characters, conflicts, problem-solving strategies, and surprise endings in stories.

- Speak and write about self and others. Add personal information to a class chart that models an oral history format.

- Write, share, and teach something new in sequence, such as a simple game or invention created in small groups. Describe its purpose and the materials, space, and time needed for completing the task.

- Use correct cursive handwriting forms in all written work. Maintain and use manuscript handwriting forms appropriately.

- Use a friendly letter format to write, revise, and edit reports with two or more paragraphs of something observed firsthand.

- Learn why and how the Dewey Decimal System is used for classifying library materials.

- Use at least three different reference sources for basic research of a single topic. Cluster and organize the information prior to writing a first draft. Share, revise, and edit based on peer feedback.

- State main idea and supporting details found in literary or subject area text. Suggest synonyms for sensory-descriptive vocabulary taken from the same text.

- Identify contractions, compound words, synonyms, antonyms, homonyms, and possessives.

- Develop questions about literary and subject area activities for peers to research and respond to.

- Participate in small groups to research and response to peer survey questions about literary and subject area issues.

- Suggest new titles for literary or subject area text. Suggest titles for peer writing efforts. Explain rationale for suggestions.

- Use alphabetic sequence and guide words when locating key words in reference materials.

- Discuss literal meanings of figurative and idiomatic language found in literature. Use different literary examples of figurative-idiomatic language as models for writing by creative imitation.

> **Reading is to the mind what exercise is to the body.**
> —Sir Richard Steele

- Make predictions about sequence, about activities, or about language patterns in stories after hearing only the first page or section of text. Confirm by further listening or reading. Evaluate accuracy or inaccuracy of predictions.

- Compare and contrast features and attitudes of characters, plots, settings, and conflicts discovered in literary selections.

- Write new beginnings or endings for favorite stories. Give characters new descriptors and behaviors opposite from those in the original story.

- Compare and contrast two or more versions of familiar folklore or of familiar folk songs having the same title. Create other versions.

- Use multimedia technology for storing, retrieving, sharing, and developing new vocabulary, new ideas, and new information found during research.

- Locate, interpret, and orally summarize simple graphs, timelines, and pictorial maps discovered during research, and as found in at least three different types of reference works.

- Identify story language patterns found in different literary titles by the same author. Compare and contrast words and phrases as exactly the same and as almost the same.

- Recognize grammatical conventions such as subject–verb agreement, use of verb tenses, composition of words (prefixes, suffixes, syllables), and the functions of nouns, verbs, adjectives, and adverbs.

- Recognize and use standard conventions in writing such as complete sentences, supporting details in paragraphs, correct spelling, correct mechanics, and correct syntax.

- Write simple letters and address envelopes correctly.

- Participate in all stages of the writing process— prewriting, drafting, receiving responses, revising, editing, and postwriting.

Reading/Writing Workshop

Many teachers integrate the reading and writing processes in third grade by creating a Reading/Writing Workshop. As part of the workshop students read books, write summaries of the books, and create a project with writing and visual or performing arts elements for presentation to the class. A workshop format can help you integrate many curricular areas in a lengthy time block. It can free your students to work at their own pace, challenging them to think, plan, and implement plans with as much or as little direction as they need, and frees you to work with students individually or in small groups.

There are several models to use for reading in your classroom—guided reading, shared reading, and independent reading.

Guided Reading

In guided reading you read with students. You can work with students individually or in groups. There are several ways to create the groups. One way is to create ability-level groupings. The advantage of ability-level grouping is that it is easier for you to plan activities if you are working in a skill-based format. The disadvantage of ability-level groupings is that no matter how you try to disguise the nature of the groups with cute names, your students will know which groups are higher level and which are lower level. Creating ability-level groupings can have a bad effect on the morale of your class, and the students who aren't reading well yet.

> **TIP!**
>
> *Give each student a gallon-sized zip-locking plastic bag in which to keep his or her Guided Reading books. Use permanent marker to label the bag with the student's name, school, and room number.*

Another way to create groups is at random. Here you risk creating difficult groups to work with in terms of their dynamics. A third way to create groups is to create different groups at different times—membership in any particular group can vary depending on what areas you feel students need to strengthen. Perhaps you notice that several students are having difficulty understanding what they read. You would form a group to focus on reading comprehension.

Guided reading allows you to listen to students read books and to closely monitor progress. The student can produce written and oral work related to what has been read in the guided-reading group. While guided-reading groups are meeting, other students in the class can work on workshop projects or work that you assign.

Shared Oral Reading

Every day you should spend some time reading aloud to your class. Shared oral reading can be used to introduce or support themes or new activities, provide background information, practice reading strategies, or for the sheer pleasure of reading. Read aloud each day to your class for about twenty minutes. Choose classic children's stories or contemporary classics that will hook your students into the joys of great writing. Read books that some students might have difficulty reading on their own, but will enjoy. Pick some of your childhood favorites or consult with your school or local librarian. Some suggestions include: *A Wrinkle in Time* by Madeline L'Engle (BDD Books, 1976), *Chitty-Chitty-Bang-Bang* by Ian Fleming (Knopf Books, 1989), *Walk Two Moons* by Sharon Creech (Harper Collins, 1994), *The Indian in the Cupboard* series by Lynne Reid Banks (Avon, 1995), and *The Forgotten Door* by Alexander Key (Scholastic, 1986).

Many people can listen more effectively if they are allowed to doodle or draw at the same time they are listening. You may find some of your students are such listeners.

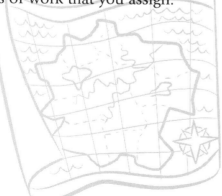

Independent Reading

D.E.A.R. Time

D.E.A.R. time means Drop Everything And Read time. Many schools recommend or require D.E.A.R. time. If yours doesn't, you may wish to implement it in your classroom. During D.E.A.R. time the only activity going on in your room is reading. Your students read, classroom visitors read, and you read.

Sustained Silent Reading (SSR)

Sustained Silent Reading is time that students devote to reading. Depending on your schedule and your students' abilities, you will want this period to last 20–30 minutes. The room should be quiet and the students encouraged to read books for the duration of the SSR period. SSR can make an excellent entry task.

Writing Conferences

During the writing workshop time, hold writing conferences with each student. Try to meet with each student every week. The length of the conference should be determined by the needs of the students, where they are in the writing process, and how much time you have in your language arts schedule. During the conference, follow these guidelines.

- Listen to the student.

- Follow the student as he or she reads the work.

- Respond to the content of the writing first, mechanics second.

- Work on one area needing improvement at a time.

Revision

There are several methods to handle the revision process. One method is to have all the revision interaction centered around you. You meet with the student in the writing conference, make comments and suggestions, and then he or she revises based on your comments.

Another method is to have your students present their works in progress to several other students individually or at the same time. Constructive comments are used to assist in the revision process by the author-presenter. Provide students with copies of the student review sheets found on page 29 to use during student writing conferences.

At intervals through the month, schedule presentations where students will present their work. Allow only constructive criticism to the author about his or her work. Involve students in the assessment process by having them write the grade they would assign to the work along with a comment on a quarter sheet of paper that you see first and then pass on.

> **TIP!**
>
> After each writing assignment, tell students to "Call in the COPS!"
> C= Check for capital letters
> O= Check for organization and order
> P= Check for punctuation
> S= Check for spelling and sense

The Writing Process

- Prewriting—getting ideas on paper

- Drafting—rough draft stage

- Revising—reviewing and changing work

- Proofreading—correcting spelling, syntax, and mechanical errors

- Publishing—creating the final copy

- Sharing—presenting the work

Workshop Project Ideas

Workshop projects can include projects with a strong writing component or projects that demonstrate understanding of the material read. Some projects your students could do include rewriting a story changing point of view, making the puppets for a puppet play of a story, making a diorama about the information in the story, writing a research paper, or building and demonstrating a model of some aspect of the story.

See-through Stories

Show your students how to create stories that build! Cut clear acetate transparency sheets in half and give four to each student. Tell students they will be creating a picture story that has four parts or events in the same setting. The first sheet will set the story, and subsequent pictures will build it. Students may want to sketch their ideas first on paper to choose the most important moments to illustrate. They may also want to make detailed drawings of their first pictures on paper to trace onto the acetate in color when ready. Detailed character drawings could be drawn on separate sheets as well.

On the first sheet have each student use permanent marker to draw or trace the settings and any characters or objects needed in the first scene. When the first drawing is done, have the student place the next sheet of acetate directly on the first one. The student draws whatever new components he or she wants to add onto the second sheet of acetate. The third and fourth sheets are done the same way. Have the student put tape across the top of the sheets so they can be flipped through like a notepad.

Create the following model on transparency sheets so that students can see the elements.

Draw a house on the bottom sheet.

Draw a tree on the second sheet.

Add a little pig by the door of the house on the third sheet.

Finally, draw a wolf coming down the street on the top sheet.

When the See-through Stories are finished, let students stand beside an overhead projector and present their stories. The students can narrate the stories as they flip through the scenes. This activity is a good way to reinforce story sequencing, introductions, conclusions, and continuity skills.

Stand-up Stories

Each Stand-up Story project requires a sheet of light-colored construction paper, scissors, paste, colored pencils or markers, and extra sheets of construction paper. The student folds the light-colored sheet of construction paper in half twice, and reopens it. He or she colors the background of the scene on the top half of the sheet, then cuts on the fold of the lower half to the middle point of the sheet. The two cut sections are overlapped and pasted together so that the scene stands up.

Characters or objects from the book are drawn on separate sheets of construction paper and cut out, leaving a flap of extra paper at the bottom. The flaps are folded under and pasted into the scene so that the characters or objects are standing upright. A summary of the book is pasted to the back of the stand-up story.

See-through Story Sample

bottom layer

top layer

Students can also use this format to illustrate historical events or to show an understanding of scientific processes they have learned. The student could portray an event such as the first Thanksgiving or a process such as the water cycle and include a brief description of what happened on the back of the scene.

Write a Hamburger Story!

Draw on the board a side view of a fat hamburger in a bun with lettuce, tomato, a thick onion slice, a layer of ketchup, and a thick pickle slice. Have each student copy the hamburger picture onto a large 12" x 18" piece of construction paper, filling the page. This will be used as a graphic outline of a story. On the top bun, the student writes an interesting introductory paragraph that grabs the reader. On the lettuce, tomato, onion, ketchup, pickle, and meat, the student writes details that add information. You could assign specific details to the ingredients such as the plot (meat), the main characters (tomato), the problem/conflict (pickle), the setting (lettuce), other characters (ketchup), and the sequence of events (onion). On the bottom bun, the student writes a concluding paragraph that ends the story. Have the student write a story based on the hamburger outline.

Shadow Plays

Prepare for this activity by drawing the outlines of characters and settings from favorite stories, and cutting them out to use as silhouettes on the overhead projector. An example of this activity comes from *Charlotte's Web* by E.B. White (Harper Collins, 1990). Draw and cut out Charlotte (the spider), Wilbur (the pig), and a barn silhouette for a setting. Place the cutouts on the overhead projector. They will create shadows. Have students stand beside the overhead and manipulate the characters as they narrate the story.

For an action shadow activity, hang a sheet from the ceiling or across a chart rack and position a strong light source behind it. Let students dramatize a story or music by moving between the light source and the sheet to create a shadow play. This is especially effective with dance movements.

> There are three rules for happiness in Industry; these three rules are: A self-selected task, a self-created plan for doing that task, and freedom to use the plan.
>
> —Anonymous

Puppet Theaters

For a quick and easy puppet theater, turn a desk on its side. Have students kneel behind the desk, between its legs, and hold puppets up over the top. The audience sees only the puppets!

A removable puppet theater can be created by using the doorway to your classroom. Most doors are 36 inches wide. Buy fabric 45 inches wide and about 4 feet long. Sew or glue a 2-inch hem in the top and slip a spring-loaded curtain rod that is the same width as your door through the hem. When the puppeteers are ready, snap the rod in the open doorway and have the puppeteers stand behind the curtain. When not in use, just roll the curtain around the rod and store it in a corner or closet.

Turn Around Characters

For poetry recitation that's new and fun, have five or six students stand in a line in front of the class with their backs to the audience. Give each student one or two lines of a poem to recite. Tell students they should *not* stand in order. The first person will turn and face the audience, introduce the poem, and turn around again. The next person then turns around, recites the appropriate lines, and turns back. With practice the timing will be smooth. This is an effective way to hold the attention of the audience—they are trying to figure out who will turn around next!

Cursive Writing

In many schools and districts students begin to learn cursive writing in the third grade. Check with your principal or resource teacher about which style of cursive writing your school or district prefers.

Phonics

Your school or district may require you to teach phonics at the third grade level. Check with the principal or curriculum coordinator at your school to find out if there is a program that you are to use to teach this reading tool.

Language Arts Activities

Journals

There are many uses for journals in the classroom. ranging from personal response journals used to communicate to science and math journals used for observation and study. Students can create reading journals to record the titles and authors of the books they have read, and any comments about the book. Journals are a great way to involve students in writing. End the day with a reflection journal where each student writes about his or her day. Students could also write to you. Every day after you review the journals, you can respond to their comments, or write personal notes of encouragement to them.

Listening

Teach a mini-lesson early in the year on "How to Listen." Have students make mini-books that illustrate the following important listening skills. Have students write each listening skill underneath its illustration and title their books "Look, Think, Wait, and Ask."

1. Look at the speaker.

2. Think about what is being said.

3. Wait until the speaker is finished.

4. Ask questions about the topic, add new information, or respond to what was said.

> Everyone who remembers his own educational experience remembers teachers, not methods and techniques. The teacher is a kingpin of the educational situation. He makes or breaks programs.
>
> —Sidney Hook, <u>Education for Modern Man</u>, 1946

Rebuses

Sticker version

Collect stickers for use in a writing center. Include a variety of characters, symbols, and everyday items. Let students create short stories or sentences substituting stickers for some of the words.

The kids in our class like to play _____.

They use a _____ to hit a _____.

Students love to create stories about their favorite superheros or cartoon characters! For these projects provide variety packs of stickers.

Stamp Version

Students use rubber stamps as substitutes for words. Discount stores often have inexpensive sets of rubber stamps that center on one theme. This activity emphasizes writing and spelling sight words or high frequency words without students having to worry about spelling unknown nouns. Provide colored-ink pads to create a bright project. Remind students to include a beginning, a middle, and an end to their stories.

Partner Nouns

Students choose partners and practice using common and proper nouns. First, a student names a common noun. Then the partner names a proper noun that matches the category of the common noun. Write the following examples on the board for the partners to consult as they do the activity.

Common Noun	Proper Noun
dog	Dalmatian
planet	Mars
hero	Superman
country	Mexico

After each match the partners switch roles, so that they take turns naming the common noun and naming a matching proper noun. To add a challenge for experienced students, set a timer and ask students to see how many matches they can make in one minute. The next day have students pair up with the same partners and repeat the activity to see if they can make more matches. Your students may start to practice at home with their families so they will be prepared for the next try!

Riddle a Day!

Ask each student to write a number riddle as a homework project early in the year. Tell students to choose a number between 1 and 1,000, then write three clues to describe their number. Ask students to draw answer lines underneath their clues.

Example:

My number starts with 1.

My number is larger than 10.

My number has 2 digits.

1. _____

2. _____

3. _____

Let students take turns posting a riddle on a large piece of paper each Monday throughout the year. Have other students write their names and guesses on the paper. If no one guesses correctly, have the student who wrote the riddle add another clue and let the guessing continue on Tuesday. Proceed in this manner throughout the week until the correct answer is discovered.

Card Collections

Many children begin making collections in third grade. Prepare for this activity by asking that your students bring their collector's cards to school along with a photo of themselves to use to make a personal collector's card.

Allow a sharing time for students to talk about their collections, so that sideline discussions will not interfere with the activity.

Ask each student to select 10 to 12 cards. Ask for student volunteers who have many cards to share with those who need cards, or call hobby shops to see if they will donate or loan cards for this activity.

Ask students to sort their cards in various categories such as subject's name, alphabetical order, date, and so on.

After students are familiar with the information on the cards, have them create collector's cards about themselves. If a photo is not available, provide crayons or colored pencils so that students can draw self-portraits. Provide students with blank cards and have them make cards about themselves. Use the example below as a guide to draw a collector's card on the chalkboard. Include your information as a model for students.

Ms. Grace Smith
Third-Grade Teacher

Oak Elementary School
Surf City, California

Birthday—2/9/61

TIP!

To protect cards from wear, photocopy the cards students bring in and pass out copies for students to use during the activity.

Spelling Word by Word

Have students sit in circles of four or five. Give one student in each circle a blank index card. Tell the student to write only the first letter of one of that week's spelling words on the index card. You can announce the word first or have the student choose the word and write its first letter on the card. Then the next student gets the card and adds the word's next letter. The third student adds the next letter, and the card gets passed around the circle until the word is complete.

Good Spelling Adds Up!

Many students memorize words and spell them correctly on the weekly spelling test, and yet they misspell these same words as they write. Here's a quick fill-in game that will encourage students to practice and develop good spelling habits.

Divide the class into teams of five or six and give each team a one-foot-length of adding machine tape. Ask the class to select a category and have the first person in each team write a word that fits the category. The second person in the team should check the spelling, correct it if necessary, and then add another word from the category. The third person checks the spelling of the first two words, makes corrections, and adds another word.

The activity continues in this way until the teacher stops the game. The team with the most words spelled correctly gets to choose the recess game or another fun activity!

To add a challenge, tell students that each new word must start with the last letter of the word before it. An animal category might produce this list: *pig, goose, elephant, tiger, rat, tarantula, alligator.*

Grab a Word

Decorate a paper bag and write *Grab Bag* on it. Fill the bag with words that you want students to learn. You can use spelling, vocabulary, or unit study words. They can be words you want students to learn that day or become familiar with by the end of the week.

Have a student volunteer reach in the bag and pull out a word. The student should either act out the word as a charade, give a definition for it, or spell it out loud. The student then gets to choose a volunteer to identify the word.

Use this as a transition activity or to prepare students for a new study unit. Create a pocket chart with a pocket for every student and label pockets with the students' names. Have students put the used word strips in their pockets on the chart. This way you can see at a glance who still needs to Grab a Word!

Speaking

Some students may need to be taught how and when to speak. Providing a visual cue will help!

Tell students that there are three voice levels they should use in school. These voice levels are represented by colors. *Green* is the loud voice used only on the playground or when doing a presentation. *Yellow* is the normal voice used for class discussions and centers conversation. *Red* means quiet. It is for no-voice situations, such as when you are in an audience or when someone else is speaking. Role-play each of these voice levels as a class.

Then separate students into three groups and have each group make a large happy face out of sturdy white cardboard. Have the first group color its happy face green, the second group yellow, and the third group red. Keep these large happy faces at the front of the classroom to use as silent signals to students to indicate the proper voice for the setting. While the groups are making their happy faces, make some smaller yellow happy faces and place them at each center to remind students of the proper voice level for that area.

Syllable Safari

Discuss word rhythms and syllables with your students. Explain how to listen to the rhythm of the word to count the syllables in it.

Tell students they are syllable hunters and they are going on a "Syllable Safari." Draw a syllable search chart like the one shown below and make copies for students.

Number of syllables	Inside	Outside
1		
2		
3		
4		

Separate students into teams of three or four. Give each team a copy of the syllable search chart. Tell the teams to hunt for something in the classroom that has a one syllable name. Tell students they should write the name on the correct area of the chart when they find it. Have students continue the search until each team has found a two, three, and four syllable name.

Take the teams outside for more syllable searching. When the charts have been completed, have teams post their results or share them at group time. Review the results to check for accuracy.

As students become more skilled at identifying the syllable count of words, change the activity by setting a time limit of 10 to 15 minutes to complete the chart and shorten the time throughout the year. Or, have students complete the chart individually at school or as a homework assignment.

Happy is he who knows the reason for things.
—Virgil

Create a Class Book

Read *A My Name Is Alice* by Jane Bayer (Dial, 1984). Assign each student a letter of the alphabet. Have students create a sentence similar to one in the book using that letter. Example: *A–my name is Amy and my husband's name is Arnie, we live in Alabama, and we sell aardvarks.* Students write the sentence at the bottom of a sheet of light-colored construction paper and draw an illustration above the sentence.

Encourage students to use original phrasing, rather than copying an idea from the book. In the case of difficult letters, let the whole class become word detectives and search for great substitutes. Tell students to research the words they choose to go with their letters so that their illustrations accurately reflect their text.

Compile the pages and photocopy them for each student. Then instruct each student to design a cover for his or her copy of the book. Have each student include a title page that lists the class as the author, illustrator, and publisher (the name of your school), and a table of contents. This project may take five to ten class periods to complete. As a follow-up activity, ask students to think about the process of creating the book, identifying the most important aspects and details they would remember for making the next book.

Famous Phrases

Each student selects a famous person or a personal hero whom he or she admires. Students will draw a portrait or find a picture of that person and glue it in the center of a sheet of 8½" x 11" paper. Ask students to label parts of the person using a noun and an adjective. Encourage students to use descriptive labels such as *chubby cheeks, happy smile, strong arms, long legs,* or *pretty hair.*

> **There are only two lasting bequests we can hope to give our children. One of these is roots; the other, wings.**
>
> —Hodding Carter

Quotations

This activity will help students use quotation marks correctly and understand which words should be placed in quotations.

Provide students with word charts that contain the names of many popular food items. You should also include the words *favorite* and *said* in the spelling list for that week.

Before the activity, practice using quotation marks as a class. Ask a student a simple question, such as *What is your favorite sport?* Quote the student in writing on the chalkboard—"My favorite sport is soccer," said Gina.

Ask each student to write a short sentence about his or her favorite food as a homework assignment. Read through the sentences as a class so that students can correct mistakes. Then have each student ask three classmates what their favorite foods are and write down the quotes. Encourage students to connect the sentences into a story and add a beginning and an ending such as the following example.

Our Four-H Club went out to eat. "I like cheeseburgers and french fries," said Leon. "My favorite food is a taco," said Jody. We had a great time eating that night. Have students share their stories by reading them aloud or by making a class book.

This activity can be easily adapted to thematic units by having students ask questions such as *What is the most interesting four-legged mammal we have studied?* or *What planet would you like to visit?*

Student Review for the Writing Workshop

Name: _____ Date: _____

Name of my story: _____

Reviewer's Name: _____

The main idea of the story is _____

_____

_____

Three details from your story are _____

_____

_____

_____ Capitalization _____ Organization _____ Punctuation _____ Spelling

What I liked about your story: _____

_____

_____

Other comments: _____

_____

_____

....

Teacher: Make copies of this review sheet for your students to use as they revise their writing projects in the Writer's Workshop. See page 21 for more information.

MATHEMATICS

Skills

- Identify the place value for each digit in numbers to 10,000.

- Use expanded notation to represent numbers.

- Read and write number words to one thousand.

- Express a number to the nearest 100.

- Express a number that is 100 more or 100 less than a given number.

- Analyze, compare, and order numbers.

- Round numbers correctly.

- Master addition and subtraction facts.

- Add and subtract four-digit numbers with renaming and regrouping.

- Practice multiplication and division facts through multiples of ten.

- Practice estimation skills.

- Express fractions emphasizing the relationship of the numerator and denominator.

- Explore the concept of a fraction from part of a whole or from a number line.

- Illustrate and describe the relationships of decimals as parts of a whole.

- Investigate and express the place value of decimals.

- Estimate sums and differences of decimals and money when appropriate.

- Make change from five and ten dollars.

- Understand symmetry.

- Use geometric terminology such as point, line, shape, perimeter, area, rays, and line segments and relate them to shapes in the environment.

- Construct and describe the properties of the following geometric shapes: circle, square, triangle, rectangle, parallelogram, and trapezoid, including their diagonals, and relate them to shapes in the environment.

- Construct and describe the properties of the following solids: cone, cube, cylinder, and sphere, and relate them to shapes in the environment.

- Construct and describe parallel lines and relate them to shapes in the environment.

- Construct and then describe the diameter and radius of a circle and relate them to shapes in the environment.

- Construct and describe a right angle and find examples in the classroom.

- Estimate and verify the perimeter of polygons.

- Estimate and measure length, width, height, area, volume, and capacity in nonstandard, U.S. customary, and metric units.

- Select the most appropriate unit to measure length, weight, area, volume, and capacity.

- Tell time to the nearest minute on both analog and digital clocks.

- Use a calendar to read and locate days, weeks, months, year, and significant events.

- Express temperature: body, boiling water, and freezing water.

- Develop logical strategies for solving problems.

- Analyze, extend, and create number patterns like 2, 3, 5, 6, 8, 9 or 0, 1, 1, 2, 3, 5, 8, 13 . . . .

- Locate and record an ordered pair for a specific point on a number plane.

- Analyze and graph an ordered pair for a function.

- Make reasonable or logical conjectures with concrete materials, using such words as *and, or, if…then, all, some, none, not,* and *out of.*

- Collect, organize, display, interpret, and analyze date in concrete, pictorial, and bar graphs.

- Predict outcomes and record results of simple probability experiments.

- Use simple tables or tree diagrams to represent possible outcomes of an experiment.

- Express the operation symbol to make a number sentence true.

- Express the missing number in a number sentence to make true sentences that demonstrate commutative, associative, or distributive properties.

- Write a mathematical expression for a phrase or sentence.

- The elementary school years are crucial in a child's cognitive and affective development, and you are the central figure. You structure classroom experiences to implement the curriculum and create a supportive environment for learning to take place. In most activities, you are the guide, the coach, the facilitator, and the instigator of mathematical explorations.

- You give children the gift of self-confidence. Through your careful grouping, astute questions, appropriate tasks, and realistic expectations, each student can experience success.

- Long after they forget childhood events, your students will remember you. Your excitement and interest permeate the room and stimulate their appreciation for mathematics.

- Through your classroom practices, you promote mathematical thinking, reasoning, and understanding.

- You lay the foundation on which further study takes place. You give students multiple strategies and tools to solve problems. The questions you ask and the problems you pose can capture your students' imagination, arouse their curiosity, and encourage their creativity.

- You facilitate the building of their knowledge by giving them interesting problems to solve, which leads to the development of concepts and important mathematical ideas.

- Rules, algorithms, and formulas emerge from student explorations guided by you, the teacher of mathematics.

—Miriam A. Leiva, <u>Curriculum and Evaluation Standards for School Mathematics, Addenda Series</u>

> We must go beyond what we were taught and teach how we wish we had been taught. We must bring to life a vision of what a mathematics classroom should be . . . A richer mathematics program is also supported by an explosion of new mathematical knowledge—more mathematics has been created in this century than in all our previous history.
>
> —Miriam A. Leiva, <u>Curriculum and Evaluation Standards for School Mathematics, Addenda Series</u>

Mathematics Activities

Evaporation Computation

On a sunny day, take your class out to a cement area. If the space is dirty, you'll want to sweep it first. Provide small containers of water and large *clean* primary paint brushes about one-inch wide for each student. Have students work in pairs. Each partner "paints" a math problem on the cement. Then the partners quickly trade places to solve each other's problem. Evaporation can occur quickly depending on the sun and temperature, so you may need to try this activity in a shady area.

This activity can also take the place of a worksheet. Give each student a copy of the worksheet you would like to use, and have the students work those problems on the sidewalk. They can check each other's work and circle the correct answers. If you walk around and observe the students as they work, you can check for accuracy and help students who are having difficulty. This activity is a great way for students to review and practice for an upcoming assessment.

If you would prefer to substitute chalk for this activity, check with the staff first to make sure that you won't be breaking any school rules against writing on the blacktop.

Making Money Count

Here's a great way to encourage your students to write longer, more interesting compound sentences.

Have students write a sentence about what they do at home to earn money. While students are working, write the money-to-syllable exchange rate below on the chalkboard.

1 *syllable words are worth a penny*
2 *syllable words are worth a nickel*
3 *syllable words are worth a dime*
4 *syllable words are worth a quarter*
5 *syllable words are worth a half dollar*

Then tell them to count the syllables in each word and check the exchange rate on the board to see how much that sentence is worth. (*For example, "I earn money at home by picking watermelons and pumpkins" is worth forty-six cents.*) Provide coin manipulatives for students to determine what their sentences are worth.

Ask students to write a sentence every morning as they arrive at school. Let them start "syllable-money savings accounts." Give each student a small notebook for recording daily "deposits" of syllable money. Remind them to keep a running balance of their accounts to help them practice addition and subtraction skills.

At the end of the month, allow students to spend their syllable money at a class store stocked with trinkets from discount stores or items donated by parents.

Addition and subtraction has more meaning for students when they can imitate real-life situations. Allowing students to accumulate and spend play money gives them a concrete understanding of adding and subtracting.

Castle of Shapes

This pattern-block activity is a creative way to integrate writing, geometry, and social studies. Gather a large supply of pattern blocks. You may need to borrow from other teachers so that students in each group have enough blocks. This activity can be done in large group or small group situations.

Have each group build a flat castle using a variety of pattern-block shapes. Provide lightweight boards, sheets of sturdy cardboard, or cardboard flats that soda cans come in for groups to use for building their castles.

Each group records how many squares, triangles, octagons, or parallelograms were used to build the castle. Students write assembly directions or draw or trace the shapes before taking the castle apart so that other groups can reconstruct the same castle.

Have students cut matching paper tiles from colored paper and glue them on construction paper to resemble the pattern castles.

> **TIP!**
>
> *Try circling all the math problems students answer correctly in orange or purple ink! You will surprise and excite your students as they discover how many problems they got right.*

When groups have finished their projects, place castle directions and drawings at a center with pattern blocks or colored paper and scissors, so others can rebuild the castles.

Students can explore symmetry by making each half of the castle identical.

To add a technological twist to this activity, use computer programs such as *Bricks* from Gryphon House that allow students to participate in these same building processes.

How Did You Get That?

Give each student a few 1" x 3" self-stick notes. Write a number on the chalkboard and have each student write a math problem that would produce that number as an answer. Students may use addition, subtraction, multiplication, division, or a combination of operations to get the answer.

Tell students to write their math problems on the self-stick notes and bring them to the chalkboard. Have students group their notes by matching their math problems with others that used the same operation. When all notes are on the board, ask students which process was used most.

This activity will help you see which students can creatively use problem-solving techniques to find an answer. Encourage students to look for unique solutions.

Personalized Problems

Have students create personal word problems using names of class members in community settings. Students will enjoy writing the problems and will learn a lot about problem-solving strategies from the writing math process.

Make a classroom book of the math problems for the math center. Repeat this activity through the year. Towards the end of the year, have students organize the problems, add a title page, a table of contents, and an index, then bind the book. Each year your class can use the books from previous years, and add its own book to the collection.

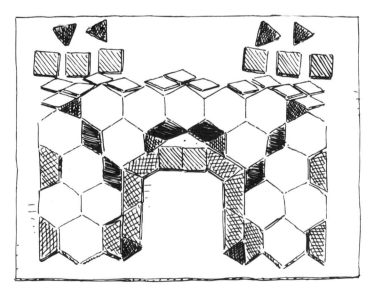

Egg-sactly Right!

Collect clean egg cartons—one for each student of your class. Use a permanent blue marker to write *Blue* on some of the cartons and a red marker to write *Red* on the others. Write one number 0–9 on the inside of each egg cup, filling in all the cups. You will repeat some numbers. In the blue cartons put four chips, pennies, or buttons. In the red cartons put three.

Show students how to close and "latch" an egg carton. Then turn it upside down and gently shake it. If you shake too hard the chips will fly out. Turn the egg carton right-side up and open it. Show students where the chips landed. Write the digits from those egg cups on the chalkboard and model how to combine them in different orders to get different number values. Have each student repeat the activity and write down as many different numbers as they can using the digits in the egg cups that had chips.

For example, if a student got 6, 3, 7, and 0 he or she could make these four-digit numbers

6,370	3,760	7,036
6,730	3,607	7,360
6,073	3,706	7,063
6,037	3,670	7,306
6,307	3,067	7,603
6,703	3,076	7,630

Have the student read the numbers aloud. As students become familiar with the activity, increase the number of chips in each egg carton.

Vary this activity by using a red, a blue, a green, and a yellow chip in each carton. The red chips are *thousands*, the blue chips are *hundreds*, the green chips are *tens*, and the yellow chips are *ones*. Students will also need a crayon in each of those colors. Students shake the cartons and write the number found in the carton, each digit in the color of the chip. For example, if the red chip landed in the egg cup marked six, six would be written in red crayon in the thousands place.

Adapting Board Games

Adapt any board game to classroom use by changing the rules. Students earn a turn by answering a math (or other subject) question. If the answer is correct, the student earns a turn; if not, the student skips a turn. Follow the rest of the board game's rules as they are normally played.

Games like *Cootie®* can be adapted to this format. To earn a leg, the student must answer a multiplication or division fact. To earn an eye, the student must answer an addition fact. To earn an antennae, the student must answer a subtraction fact, and so on. You can define the game according to what your students need to practice most.

The object of education is to prepare the young to educate themselves throughout their lives.

—Robert Hutchins

Airplane Arithmetic

Students love to make paper airplanes—so let them explore aerodynamics while practicing math facts. Give each student a sheet of paper to fold into an airplane. Call out a math fact to each student. If the student gives the correct answer, he or she can fly the plane toward a wastebasket or designated landing spot. If it is the wrong answer, the student can try again later.

Plan a Class Party!

Involve your students in planning a class party. Brainstorm as a class the menu, the ingredients, and the amounts that will be needed. Have students compile a list and research the costs at a grocery store as a homework assignment. Remind students to note the name of the grocery store and to check the quantities contained in each package as they figure how much they have to buy and how much it will cost. When they bring the information to school, compare prices to see where the best buys are and figure out how to finance the party.

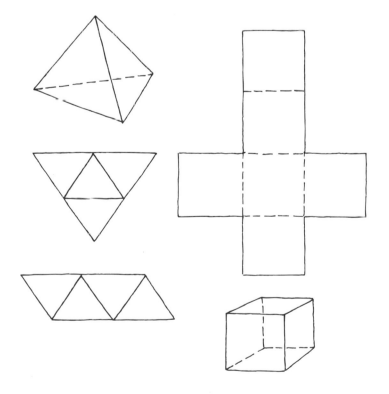

Nets

Collect numerous empty cardboard boxes of many shapes and sizes. From the collection of cardboard boxes have each student select a box to cut open so that it can be flattened into one piece. Encourage students to cut open their boxes in different ways. Have them lay out their flattened figure on a desk or table top. Tell them these figures are called nets.

Select one of the nets and ask the class to predict what kind of box could be made from it. Have one student remake the box from the net and show it to the class.

Show the class a regular tetrahedron. Ask them to visualize what the net would look like and have them draw it freehand. There are two possibilities.

Pass out copies of the worksheet on page 36. Students look at a cube and draw some of the possible nets of it. Have students cut out and fold their nets to verify whether a cube could be completed from them. Challenge them to find as many of the eleven possible nets as they can and verify by folding. Display the student solutions on the bulletin board.

Flashcards

Use the template on page 37 to make fact family flashcards. Write one factor each in the bottom two angles of the triangle. In the top angle of the triangle write the product of the two factors. For example, you would write 3 in one bottom corner, 2 in the other bottom corner, and 6 in the top angle.

The flashcards can be used in two ways—for multiplication or for division. Students cover the product in the top angle with their hands to practice multiplication. They cover one of the bottom corners to practice division facts. To continue our example from above—a student covers the 6 at the top of the triangle to practice 3 x 2 and covers the 2 in one of the bottom angles to practice 6 ÷ 3. Your students will develop much better number sense by practicing multiplication and division at the same time.

Net Grid

Teacher: Provide each student with several copies of this grid paper. Remind students that a net is what the surface of a three-dimensional object would look like if it were opened and flattened. Students look at a cube and draw some of the possible nets of it. Have students cut out and fold their nets to verify whether a cube can be completed from it. Challenge the students to find as many of the eleven possible nets as they can and verify by folding. Activity described on page 35.

Flashcard Template

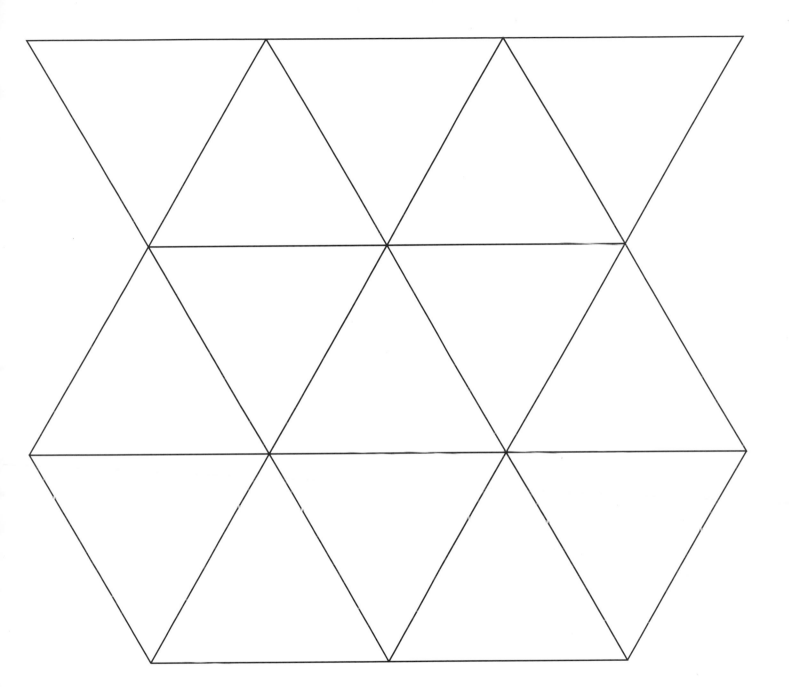

Teacher: Reproduce this page for each student. Have students cut out the flashcards and then write fact families on them, for example: 0, 0 and 12; 12, 1 and 12; 24, 2 and 12; 36, 3 and 12; 48, 4 and 12; 60, 5 and 12; 72, 6 and 12; 84, 7 and 12; 96, 8 and 12; 108, 9 and 12; 120, 10 and 12; 132, 11 and 12; and finally, 144, 12 and 12. See diagram. As you introduce each new times table, provide a new flashcard template to your students. Students use them to study multiplication and division facts by covering the number that represents the answer.

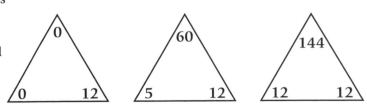

PHYSICAL EDUCATION

Skills

- **Locomotor:** hop backward; hop to a musical rhythm; jump making a half turn; jump with a long jump rope; jump rope with a partner; jump to waltz time music; skip with a definite rhythm, skip around cones on a 10-foot line; skip to music; gallop with the nondominant foot leading; slide sideways in both directions with ease; leap to an irregular drumbeat; leap while trying to rebound a basketball; change directions quickly; and dodge two thrown balls in a dodge ball game.

- **Nonlocomotor:** stretch body parts while sitting, standing, and kneeling; swing and sway the body to an advanced musical pattern; shake all parts of the body at the same time.

- **Manipulative movements:** catch a rolling ball on either side; catch a ball which has bounced off a wall before it hits the ground; catch a thrown football; bounce a ball while walking for ten feet; return a ball to a specific square by hitting it upward, using an open palm (two-square and four-square); return a handball serve; carry an object with accuracy to a defined area; pitch a rolling ball to the kicker; play a game of caroms by the rules; play a game of table golf by the rules; play a game of maze by the rules; throw a ball at a moving target in a socco game; throw a ball to make an "out" in kickball (or bootball); throw a ball using a softball throw; shoot a ball at the basket in basketball; pass a football; practice kicking a ball with accuracy; dribble a ball with the feet; play in a soccer game; dribble a ball during a basketball game; serve a volleyball; strike a rubber ball 20 feet in a fistball game; demonstrate a proper handball serve; play tetherball; understand the concept of follow-up techniques in tetherball; hit a ball with a bat off a batting tee.

> The play of shine and shade on the trees as the supple boughs wag,
>
> The delight alone or in the rush of the streets, or along the fields and hill-sides,
>
> The feeling of health, the full-noon trill, the song of me rising from bed and meeting the sun.
>
> —Walt Whitman, Song of Myself

- **Perceptual motor skills:** listen to and repeat a sequence of movements on command; listen to and practice acting out complex cues given on a record, tape, or CD.

- **Rhythm and dance:** practice the bleking step and the slide step.

- **Flexibility and agility:** complete a challenge course involving twisting and bending; perform several stunts on the apparatus.

- **Muscular strength and endurance:** participate in hanging and climbing activities; use the circular traveling rings; perform a variety of stunts on the horizontal ladder; perform the flexed-arm hang; perform pull-ups; perform 20 modified sit-ups.

- **Cardiorespiratory endurance:** follow a complex course by running, jumping, and dodging; be aware of one's limitations to prevent excessive fatigue; jog for four to five minutes (some walking is permitted).

- **Balance:** balance on either foot with eyes closed; walk a line backward, toe to heel, for five feet; walk a balance beam, heel to toe, forward and backward.

- **Self-image enhancement:** realize when one's personal performance is successful; serve as a leader of a squad or team during a skill activity; recognize that practice may be necessary to attain goals; move to the rhythm of a poem; exhibit feelings and emotions through movement.

- **Social behavior:** accept majority decisions gracefully; accept suggestions from others; clarify the rules of games so there is common understanding; invent a game with a group; demonstrate a game or stunt; give one's best effort when losing.

- **Leadership:** serve as equipment monitor; assume the roles of captain, squad leader, or referee as needed; lead the class in an exercise.

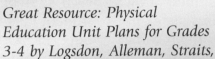

TIP!

Great Resource: Physical Education Unit Plans for Grades 3-4 by Logsdon, Alleman, Straits, Belka and Clark (Human Kinetics, 1986)

students may choose to do on the playground. You can't guide students in settling disputes unless you are aware of the rules that were originally taught.

The PE program can enhance a unit you teach in your classroom as well. For example, as third graders explore an *Animals of the Night* section of a Light unit, the PE teacher might include an obstacle course based on the movements of bats. Explore the possibilities that coordinated teaching provides.

Teaching Physical Education

If you teach your own physical education classes, you will want a balanced program that includes the skills listed at the beginning of this physical education section. Talk with other third-grade teachers about how and when their students participate in this subject. If you enjoy teaching sports and physical fitness and aren't as comfortable with music, you may find another teacher who will exchange these subjects with you—you teach her students physical education and she teaches your students music, or vice versa.

Most important to keep in mind, is that physical education is an important part of a balanced scholastic program. There are students who may not be as comfortable in traditional academic subjects, but who excel in physical education activities. Knowing their strengths can give you the key to helping them in the classroom.

Depending on the nature of your students you may want to have a short PE period every day of twenty minutes or so, or twice a week for 40–50 minutes.

Many schools employ specialists in the area of physical education. Visit with that teacher and work collaboratively to enhance both of your programs. The PE teacher will appreciate your reinforcement of class activities during recess periods. It is important for you to know the rules that are taught during PE class for games the

Sports

Some team sports appropriate for developing third-grade physical education skills are bootball (or kickball), volleyball, baseball, basketball, relay races, and field hockey. Some individual sports are dodge ball, four square, volleyball, handball, tetherball, and gymnastics.

Physical Education Activities

Four Square

You will need a four square court where students will practice serving, hitting, and rotating. Introduce the game and explain the rules. Show students the court set-up. The player in square one is always the server and serves from behind the serve line. To serve the ball, drop and hit it underhanded after the first bounce. If the ball hits a line, the server is out. The player who receives the ball can direct it with an underhand hit to any square. Play continues until one player fails to return the ball or commits a fault.

Four Square Faults

- hitting the ball overhand or sidearm

- landing the ball on the line between the squares

- stepping into another square to play the ball

- catching or carrying a return volley

- allowing the ball to touch any part of the body except the hands

When a player misses or commits a fault, he or she moves to the end of the waiting line, and the players on the court move to fill empty squares, leaving the fourth square open. The person at the head of the line moves into square four to become a player.

Circle Jump

Have students stand in a circle. The leader stands in the center of the circle holding a long jump rope. The leader carefully moves the rope close to the ground in a long, low circle, and as it reaches each student, he or she hops over the rope. If a student fails to make it over the rope, he or she is out. The last person still in the circle is the next leader. Students must keep the rope very low for safety. If there is a painted circle in the gymnasium or on the playground, have students stand on it to hold the circle shape better.

Cat-and-Mouse Games

Third graders love the thrill of the chase. Cat-and-mouse games are right up their "alley!"

Streets and Alleys

One student is the mouse and another is the cat. All of the other students line up in rows of four so that when their arms are outstretched, their fingers just touch. Stand at the front of the rows and explain that when students are facing you they are making streets, and when they turn to the right and touch fingers they are making alleys. The cat can only chase the mouse up and down the streets and alleys. The cat cannot cut between, the mouse can.

Start with students facing you. Call out "Streets." The cat chases the mouse. Then call out "Alleys," and have students turn to the right. Now the cat and mouse run through the alleys. Call "Streets" again after a short time. If the cat catches the mouse within the time limit you set, then a new mouse is chosen. If the cat can't catch the mouse during that time, a new cat and mouse are chosen.

Hills and Valleys

This cat-and-mouse game resembles Streets and Alleys, but in this version students stand in a circle holding hands. Call out "Hills," and have students raise their arms. The cat tries to catch the mouse by running in and out of the circle under the raised arms. Call out "Valleys," and students lower their arms. The chase continues around the circle. If the cat catches the mouse within the time limit, a new mouse is chosen. If not, both students get to choose a new cat and mouse.

SCIENCE AND HEALTH

Science

- Explore, observe, and examine objects using a combination of senses to collect, compare, organize, and interpret data.

- Identify basic characteristics when recording observations and when classifying or ordering objects or events.

- Suggest possible reasons as to why and how events have taken place.

- Make predictions based on prior knowledge.

- Design or plan appropriate investigations to support or refute a hypothesis.

- Generate data by investigating; record data in words, pictures or graphs; and organize data by classifying or arranging in sequential order.

- Compare relative weights, distances, and volumes.

- Use metric and U.S. customary systems of measurement.

- Analyze, compare, evaluate, interpret, report, and apply data, and reach judgements about situations or events.

- Summarize experiences and apply them.

- Select and follow directions safely in manipulating science materials.

- Provide and maintain optimum environments for plants and animals.

- Utilize appropriate reading and language skills in comprehending science content.

- Develop and use a science vocabulary.

- Describe how technology and science-related careers have affected our lives.

Science Center

Create an easily accessible space in your room for basic science equipment, such as magnifying glasses, eye droppers, string, a microscope, gram weights, thermometers, a balance scale, rulers, paper, pencils, crayons, and scissors. You will also need "specimen" containers (plastic boxes, shoe boxes, or plastic bowls with lids). Invite students to add to this science center all year. Encourage students to donate interesting things found during playground time or nature walk discoveries.

Add reference books, magazine articles, maps, charts, and examples of items that relate to new units of studies. For earth science studies add cups of different kinds of soil; for health science studies add the food pyramid or models of body systems; for life science units add plants, seeds, an ant farm, or a mealworm habitat; and for physical science add simple machines such as levers, screws, wedges, and pulleys.

Establish a bulletin board near the science center for current events that emphasize scientific study. Encourage students to bring in news clippings for posting on the board. Some possible subjects are weather-related stories, reports of space exploration, or the discovery of fossils. As students contribute information, discuss how it affects their lives. Does this event hold promise as a cure for cancer? How does a volcanic eruption somewhere affect the weather in our part of the world? Provide students with more information by accessing news sites on the Internet or assist them in a search on that subject.

> **Learning science is something that students do, not something that is done to them. "Hands-on" activities are not enough. Students must have "minds-on" experiences as well.**
>
> **—National Science Education Standards**

> ### The whole of science is nothing more than a refinement of everyday thinking.
>
> —Albert Einstein, <u>Physics and Reality</u>, 1936

Science Safety

Keep dangerous or hazardous materials out of the hands of students.

Supervise every experiment. Use small groups if necessary.

Learn first aid and have a first-aid kit readily available.

Require students to report accidents or injuries while experimenting.

Caution students not to perform experiments at home without a parent or adult present.

Teach students how to thoroughly wash hands after handling animals, chemicals, or other potentially dangerous substances.

Set up a data bank that includes maps, a globe, solar system charts, an atlas, a dictionary, science texts, old National Geographic magazines, science-themed puzzles, charts, and any other printed matter that pertains to your science curriculum.

If you are nervous about performing scientific experiments in front of the class, try doing it alone and videotaping it first. If anything goes wrong, you can solve the problem and retape. The videotape is a great help for students who were absent or had difficulty conducting the experiment alone. The tape can even go home for homebound students to watch. Videotapes of students performing experiments can be shown to parents at Open House.

Invite experts to your class to discuss their areas of expertise. Potential scientific visitors are colleagues with special knowledge or community resource people. This helps students relate classroom learning to the world outside the walls.

Know, Want to Learn, Learned!

Create KWL (Know, Want to Learn, Learned) charts with your students at the beginning of each new unit. Use butcher paper or large sheets of construction paper to create the chart. Announce the topic of study or theme to students. In the first column or on the first sheet write *Know* in large letters. Ask students what they know about the subject and write their responses on the chart, even if it is not factually correct. In the second column or on the second sheet write *Want to Learn*. Ask students what they want to learn about this subject and record their responses on the chart. Leave the *Learned* section blank during the introduction phase of the unit. Keep the KWL chart(s) posted during the unit. Add to the *Learned* section as you finish different lessons, or as students make important discoveries.

Know	Want to Learn
Hawaii has volcanos.	What makes volcanos erupt?
Mt. St. Helens was a volcano.	What comes out of a volcano?
Volcanos kill people.	

Help students develop experiments to discover the answers to their questions. When you have finished the topic, review the *Learned* section and add any important conclusions students reach.

The Scientific Process

Prepare a chart for the wall or desk markers for students list the steps of the scientific process. Check your curriculum or science text to assure that you use the terminology that is accepted in your school or district.

Question

Think of an interesting problem or concern, or of something you want to know about.

Hypothesize

Take a guess! Predict what you think will happen when you conduct the experiment. Why do you think this will happen? You may want to ask others what they think.

Test

Try your idea. You may need to try it more than once to check the results. Try the experiment in different ways, but control the variables to assure accuracy.

Observe

Use all your senses as you make the discoveries. Record any information or data that you collect. Document it in a way that makes sense to you.

Conclude

Did your data help you reach a conclusion? Are you sure about the conclusion? Would you change anything you did? Did your conclusion match your hypothesis? (Be sure students understand that the conclusion may or may not match the hypothesis.)

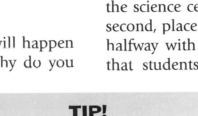

TIP!

Write to the National Science Teachers Association, 1742 Connecticut Avenue, N.W., Washington, DC 20009 for great help in teaching science.

Physical Science

States of Matter

A quick way to demonstrate the states of matter is to place an ice cube in an empty, clean tuna can. As a cube, it is a *solid*. When it melts, it is a *liquid*. When you place the tuna can on a warming tray (adult supervision required) and it evaporates, it is a *gas*.

Place three identical yogurt containers with lids at the science center. In the first, place rocks; in the second, place nothing; and fill the third container halfway with water. Secure the lids with tape so that students cannot peek inside. Number the containers. Inform students that one container holds a solid, one holds a gas, and one holds a liquid. Tell students to identify which containers holds each state of matter. After all students have had an opportunity to determine the contents of the containers, remove the lids and reveal what is inside each container.

Try the activity again, replacing the rocks with cotton balls. See how the results change!

Changes in Matter

Explain to students that matter can change in two ways—*physical* change and *chemical* change.

Physical change can be demonstrated by giving each student a ball of play dough or clay. Ask students to transform the balls into snakes of clay. Point out that they have made a physical change in the clay. Students can also tear a piece of paper into tiny pieces to demonstrate this principle. The form has changed, but it is still paper.

Chemical change can be demonstrated by burning a piece of paper. Chemical changes cause the item to take on different characteristics than the original matter. Rust on metal is a chemical change in the metal.

Mystery Matter

Place half a box of cornstarch in a bowl and add water, stirring it slowly and mixing well. To add to the mystery, add one to three drops of food coloring to the mixture. It usually takes less than a cup of water, but the amount can vary so experiment. The mixture should not be runny, it should flow when you pick it up and break off as well. It will have the properties of a solid and a liquid. Ask students which type of matter it is. Explore student responses. Afterwards, seal the mixture in a bowl. When you want to use it again, add a drop of water to revive it.

Life Science

Introduce life science to your students by letting them observe many different examples of living things in your classroom.

Classroom Animals

Some students may have small pets their families will loan to your class for a short period of time. Your school or district may have a discretionary budget you can use to purchase inexpensive animals like fish, chameleons, or hamsters. Provide the proper habitat for each animal and be sure the animal has no diseases which can transfer to your students. Turtles make great classroom pets, but some carry diseases such as salmonella. If you allow a turtle into your class, have a veterinarian give it a clean bill of health and insist that students wash their hands thoroughly after they handle it.

Classroom Plants

Display a variety of plants in your classroom. Unusual ones such as the Venus Flytrap, which catches insects, or the Spider plant, which sends out tendrils resembling spiders, are great to watch. Insert toothpicks in a yam, sweet potato, or an avocado or mango pit and suspend it in a jar of water so students can observe root growth. If you use a yam, check with your grocer to be sure it has not been radiated to prevent root growth.

Sprouting Seeds

Give each student a zippered sandwich bag, a bean seed, a radish seed, and a damp paper towel. Have students write their names on the bags with permanent markers. Have students fold their paper towels, insert them in the bags, and position the seeds on the towels. Now tape each bag onto a sunny window and wait a few days to see what happens. Students will be delighted to watch germination occur and sprouts appear. For contrast, hang some extra bags in a dark closet. Let students compare these seeds with those in the sunny window to see if germination occurs and if these seeds sprout and grow. Students will quickly realize that seeds do not need sunlight for germination, but they do need sunlight to grow.

Terrarium-Create a Habitat

Students construct terrariums out of two two-liter soda pop plastic containers. Remove the labels from the bottles, cut the top two-thirds off one bottle and the top half off the second. Recycle the pieces with the bottle necks. Poke 8–12 air holes in the half-bottle and make three one-inch slits at the rim so that it will slide into the ⅓ bottle. Cut a door in the side that can be opened and easily resealed.

> **The world looks so different after learning science.**
>
> **For example, trees are made of air, primarily. When they are burned, they go back to air, and in the flaming heat is released the flaming heat of the sun which was bound in to convert the air into tree. [A]nd in the ash is the small remnant of the part which did not come from air, that came from the solid earth, instead.**
>
> **These are beautiful things, and the content of science is wonderfully full of them. They are very inspiring, and they can be used to inspire others.**
>
> **—Richard Feynman**

Place a layer of sand or gravel in the bottom, add soil and a bit of gardener's charcoal. Add a local plant or two. Water soil well. Slide the top into the base.

Have students collect insects from the school area to populate their terrariums. Remind students to seal the flap door after placing the creatures and food inside, and watch how they live, move, and interact.

Observe the terrarium and take notes in an observation log over a period of time. Discuss what students have learned about habitats over the course of the experience.

Cup o' Grass

This activity is sure to cause some hair-raising fun! Give each student a plastic foam cup and permanent markers. Tell students to draw a face on the cup. Then let students fill their cups with soil and sprinkle grass seed on the top. Have them pat the seed down and sprinkle water on top. Set the cups in a warm place and keep them moist, but not soaked. Soon grass will sprout and begin to grow. When the "cup characters" get a good head of grass growing, let students give them a "hair cut!"

Have students care for and observe the cup characters for a few weeks. Point out for students that just as a lawn grows, the cells of the living grass in their cups respond to their environment and grow. Let students create wild styles with the grass "hair!"

Fill the bottom of a gift box or a cardboard softdrink flat with a layer of fine sand about a half-inch deep. Ask students to bring small toy houses, fences, animals, or trees from home. Arrange them in the box.

Place the box in the center of a sheet or a vinyl tablecloth. Aim a small fan or hair dryer on low speed at the diorama, holding it about three feet away. Let it blow for 10–15 seconds. Observe the new landscape. Collect the sand that blew away and measure it. Let students rearrange the toy items and reposition them so that less "soil" is lost.

TIP!

Use your web browser to search for elementary science list servers and web sites. These sites often include lesson plans prepared by experienced classroom teachers.

Earth Science

Wind Erosion

Preview this activity by discussing wind erosion. Show pictures and explain how conservationists attempt to terrace the land, use trees to create wind breaks, and plant cover crops in order to prevent loss of topsoil. Students can use this background information in designing a diorama to prevent wind erosion.

> The function of thinking is not just solving an actual problem but discovering, envisaging, going into deeper questions. Often in great discoveries the most important thing is that a certain question is found. Envisaging, putting the productive question is often more important, often a greater achievement than solution of a set question.
>
> —M. Wertheimer, <u>Productive Thinking</u>, 1945

Water Erosion

Fill an old cookie sheet with soil and sprinkle grass seed on it a week before you plan to do this experiment. When the seed has sprouted, begin the experiment. Fill another old cookie sheet with only soil and prop one end up on books. Place the other end in a collection tub. Pour a small pitcher of water onto the top end of the cookie sheet and watch how much soil ends up in the tub. Conduct the same experiment in exactly the same way with the grassy cookie sheet. The grass will protect the soil so that not as much is lost to erosion.

Friction

Have students collect several different kinds of rocks and classify them by color, size, shape, texture, and type. Use library resources to accurately identify what types of rocks they are. Select two porous or crumbly rocks. Have students rub the two rocks together over a dark piece of paper. Examine the tiny particles that fall on the paper with a magnifying glass. Students will discover that soil is actually made up of tiny pieces of rock that have been weathered and worn over many years.

Food-Chain TV

Write *OWL* at the top of the chalkboard or on chart paper. Ask students, *If you were an owl, what would you like for dinner?* Accept any reasonable answer, such as a snake. Write *SNAKE* on the chart below owl. Then ask *What would a snake like for dinner?* If mouse is the answer, write *MOUSE* below snake on the chart. Finally, ask students *What would a mouse like for dinner?* If the answer is seeds, write *SEEDS* on the chart. Your students have just created a food chain!

Separate students into small groups and let them create other food chains. Tell students they can start at the top of the food chain and work down, or at the bottom and work their way up the chain. Let each group present its food chain to the class. Guide students through any corrections that need to be made.

Ask each student to bring a small shoe box to school. Have each student cut a window in the bottom of his or her box, then turn the box on its side and poke holes through both sides large enough to fit short dowels. Ask each student to select a food chain to illustrate on adding machine tape. Show students how to draw each picture so that they will show in the window or "TV screen" of the box one at a time. Remind students to draw the pictures in the order of the food chain. For each box attach the leader paper and the end paper of the adding machine tape to the dowels and glue them in place. Roll the tape onto one dowel and slowly turn the opposite dowel to unroll the tape and reveal the Food-Chain TV program. Let students narrate their food-chain stories as they are shown.

HEALTH

Skills

Personal health: Maintain appropriate health, grooming, and cleanliness standards; recognize how health is affected by daily health habits and prompt attention to symptoms of illness; identify signs of self-acceptance and acceptance of others, including the handicapped; relate increased physical activity to increase in pulse/breathing rates; recognize relationship of rest and sleep to individual performance; participate in activities to strengthen the body and maintain good posture.

Family health: Demonstrate methods of support and respect for other family members; compare ways in which each family member depends on other family members; describe how the life cycle involves growth, development, and the aging process; recognize that in order for the life cycle to continue, things must reproduce; explain ways in which environment influences the development of living organisms; discuss parenting and ways in which parents care for their young.

Nutrition: Use food groups as a guide in daily food choices; identify and use snacks that are low in sugar and salt; analyze effects of overeating and undereating on physical health and well-being; recognize need to include vegetables, fruit, and fibrous foods in the diet; explain role of people who produce, process, market, and prepare foods; identify cleanliness practices related to handling and storing foods.

Mental/emotional health: Identify and describe positive and negative feelings; determine and respond to the emotional state of another person; relate ways that help one get along with others, including adults; identify ways to reduce stress; enumerate steps in making a decision; accept responsibility for one's actions.

> **Be true to your teeth, and they won't be false to you.**
>
> —Soupy Sales

Use and misuse of substances: Differentiate between helpful or harmful substances; predict the effect of certain drugs on physical, mental, and social functioning; explain the importance of taking only prescribed medications; recognize, refuse, and report offers of known or unknown substances to a parent, teacher, or other trusted adult.

Diseases and disorders: Differentiate between communicable diseases and chronic diseases; recognize how germs may enter the body; cooperate with parents, teachers, and medical personnel to protect and maintain health.

Consumer/community and environmental health: Discriminate between reliable (physician, nurse, parent, teacher) and unreliable (media, friends) sources of health information; analyze reasons for choosing or not choosing commonly-used health products; identify community health workers and the importance of their services, identify personal responsibilities in maintaining a healthful environment at home, school, and the community-at-large; describe how a safe, healthful environment improves the quality of life.

Safety, accident prevention, and emergency services: Differentiate between good and bad touching, list steps to take if one is touched inappropriately; take precautions for self-protection in public places; describe situations that may be safe or unsafe; discuss how to prepare for an emergency; identify ways to prevent accidents in and around home; recognize and demonstrate appropriate behavior during school emergency drills.

47

Health Activities

Super Sources

Health resources could include local home economists, family- and consumer-education agents, school nurses, and Four-H Clubs or Scouting programs that offer health projects. Food-producing corporations offer informative brochures through their web sites or the toll-free telephone numbers on their products.

Parent Education

Let students educate their parents about the food pyramid, the food groups, and the daily requirements that are recommended now. When students are comfortable with their healthy food-fact knowledge, send copies of the food pyramid home with students and ask them to explain it to their parents.

Potluck

Read *Potluck* by Anne Shelby (Orchard Books, 1991). Create a class alphabet chart by allowing each student to name a food that begins with the first letter of his or her name. Then let each student create a potluck menu for his or her family using the first letter in each family member's name to select a food.

To extend the idea, ask each student to choose ten friends to come to dinner and list the food items that could be brought using their names.

Give each student a blank copy of the food pyramid. Explain to students that each item at their potluck dinners should fit into one of the food groups. Work with students to determine if the potluck dinners they hosted provided well-balanced meals.

Use and Misuse of Substances

Talk to students about smoking, alcohol, and drugs. Talk about what each of these does to your body. Discuss the benefits of prescribed medicine when used correctly. Discuss what students should do if someone offers them any of these substances, or any substances with which they are not familiar.

Write situations on cards posing dilemmas students could face. Have students choose a partner. Students draw cards and role play the situation on the card. A card could provide a situation like this sample. "An older girl at school offers you a cigarette. What do you do?"

Recycling

Teach students the importance of recycling. Talk about why recycling is necessary. Brainstorm a list of items that can be recycled. Start recycling in your own classroom. Place cardboard boxes around the room with labels for paper, cans, and bottle recycling. Talk to the students about where the items are taken and how they are recycled.

Clean Up Litter

Take a walking field trip to a local park. Sit in a circle with your class and discuss the surroundings. Talk about litter, what it does to our environment, and what students can do about it. If the park is messy, have students pick up trash, and throw it away and/or collect recyclables. The students are doing their parts to care for the environment. After the students have finished, sit in a circle and talk about their experiences. Brainstorm ways that the students could make the community more aware of the importance of a clean environment. Possible ideas could be holding a can drive, making posters for local businesses, of having a regular clean-up-the-park-day.

> It is the supreme art of the teacher to awaken joy in creative expression and knowledge.
>
> —Albert Einstein

Name: _____ Date: _____

Topic _____

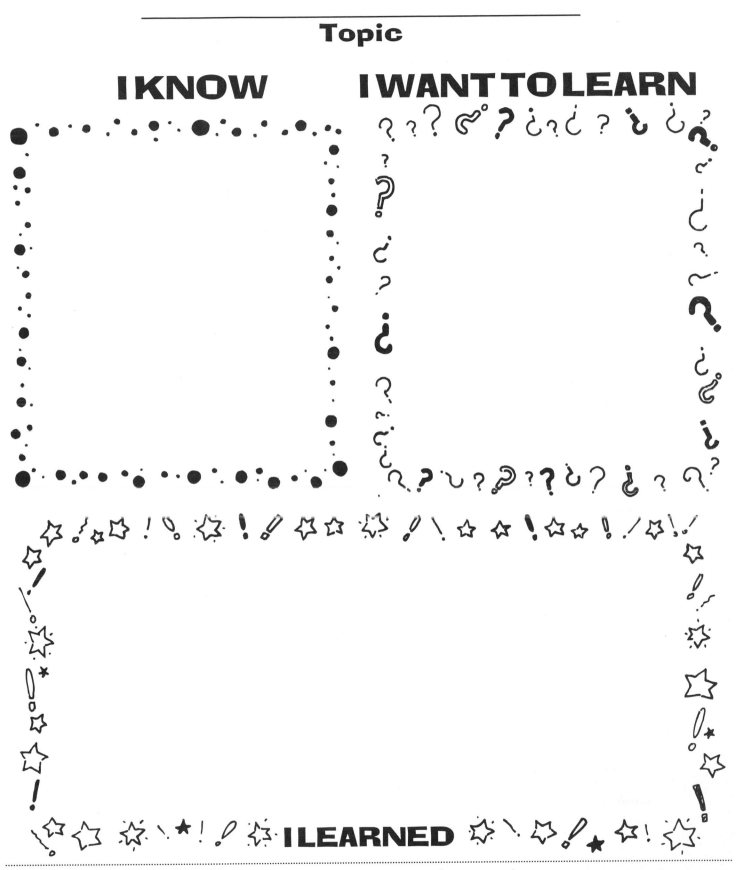

IKNOW

IWANTTOLEARN

ILEARNED

FS122005 Getting Ready to Teach Third Grade

SOCIAL STUDIES

Skills

- Information related to certain topics can be obtained from written sources such as books, newspapers, magazines, dictionaries, documents, encyclopedias, and bibliographies. Information can also be acquired from radio, television, computer software, film, and from other people.

- Listen to receive directions and explanations, expand word meanings, and comprehend and contribute ideas.

- Use the following parts of a book to find information: title page, table of contents, chapter/unit headings, index, and glossary.

- Identify traits and skills needed for various kinds of work that is done in the community.

- Provide summaries in oral and written form by writing lists and creating titles for pictures and stories.

- Answer questions related to a specific topic using complete sentences as appropriate.

- Sequence months, years, directives, processes, procedures, facts, and events.

- Prepare oral and written communication such as group letters, descriptions of persons, places, things, interests, and events.

- Conduct simple interviews with people in various careers; tell about the kind of work and their degree of personal satisfaction with their jobs.

- Create and participate in various activities, such as plays and puppet shows, involving a study of people, events, and ideas.

- Classify information about occupations and careers in the local community.

- Identify the globe as a model of the earth.

- Define the word "map" as a representation of an area.

- Compare sizes and shapes of land and water masses, and identify the continents and oceans.

- Recognize and apply map and globe concepts and terms such as hemisphere and cardinal directions (north, up, south, down, etc.).

- Identify, describe, read, and use classroom maps. Understand and use map compass, scale, and legend.

- Identify time zone changes as appropriate.

- Interpret pictures by comparing information from several different or similar pictures, and by relating words and phrases to the pictorial content.

- Submit, interpret, categorize, and classify given information to obtain data for charts, tables, graphs, diagrams, and time lines to be used in presentations to the class.

- Place chronological facts and events in sequential order for making time lines.

- Read and explain the information or message contained in various posters and in simple cartoons.

- Identify obvious stereotypes.

- Explain main ideas and supporting ideas in selected paragraphs.

- Differentiate between fact, fiction, and opinion.

- State the meaning of and interpret various concepts.

- Acquire relevant factual information and make generalizations about people and events.

- Identify problems or issues.

- Present the problem or issue in another form for further clarification.

- Objectively judge information related to the problem or issue for its consistency and relevance.

- Devise and choose a solution(s).

- Execute the solution plan.

- Evaluate the solution and draw conclusions.

- Demonstrate or express respect for justice, reverence, and love for family, and others when participating in group or individual activities.

- Clarify through discussion and/or actions an awareness of personal values.

- Identify examples of values conflicts related to home and the community.

- Demonstrate a respect for law and order.

- Demonstrate respect for the rights of others.

- Cooperate with others by setting goals for individual and group work.

- Recognize that all individuals live within a framework of rules and laws.

- Identify the various responsibilities which people assume related to home, school, and the community.

- Respect diversity by demonstrating the ability to interact cooperatively and effectively with various cultural and ethnic groups.

- Explain the importance of conservation, ecology, and resources.

- Express interest in personal heritage.

> **Students need more than facts. They need to understand the relationships between "facts" and whose interests certain "facts" serve. They need to question the validity of the "facts," to ask questions such as "why" and "how." They need to know how to find information, to solve problems, to express themselves in oral and written language so their opinions can be shared with, and have an influence on, broader society. It is only through such an approach that students can construct their own beliefs, their own knowledge.**
>
> **—Bob Peterson "What Should Children Learn?: A Teacher Looks at E.D. Hirsch" in Rethinking Schools—An Agenda for Change**

Social Studies Activities

Map Puzzles

Photocopy a map of your community onto sturdy paper and laminate it. Be sure the map's scale is large and easy for third graders to read. Enlarge the map in the phone book or get one from your city's visitor's bureau or Chamber of Commerce. Cut the map into large puzzle pieces and place the pieces in an envelope for use at a geography center. You could also make puzzles from maps of other cities and locations near your area.

To extend the activity, have students draw a map of the school or their neighborhood. Model a very simple line drawing of a map on the chalkboard. Give each student a sheet of heavy construction paper, scissors, and markers. Let students create map puzzles to add to the Geography Center.

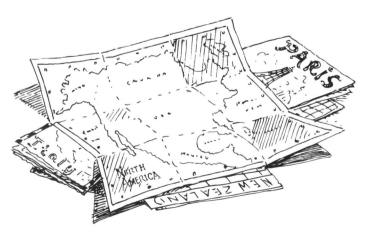

Map Center

Set up a basket with a variety of maps in it. Encourage students to spread them out on the floor and explore the details. They will have fun using a magnifying glass to get up close! When a student finds an interesting spot, have him or her record the location on a piece of paper taped to the back of each map.

When a student's family is planning a vacation, obtain a map of the area and have the student show classmates where he or she is going.

Include a world globe at the map center. If possible, include a variety of globes for students to explore and find interesting places. Trade with other teachers so there is a new globe in your center each month. Varying the materials in the center is stimulating for students.

Read a story based in another country, such as *"Mufaro's Beautiful Daughters: An African Tale"* by John Steptoe (Lothrop, 1987). Have a student locate Zimbabwe, the setting of the illustrations, and show it to the class.

Mountains Up!

Review geographical terms or unit studies vocabulary with this game, which is similar to the classic 7-Up game. Choose seven students to be "It." All other students put their heads down and hold their thumbs up. Each "It" taps a different student's thumb and then returns to the front of the room, picks up a vocabulary card, and holds it up. The students whose thumbs are tapped should quickly put them down to prevent anyone else from selecting them.

When the seven students who are "It" have returned to the front, the teacher calls out, "Heads up, Mountains up!" All students whose thumbs were tapped stand and the teacher calls on each one in turn to select the student who picked them. However, rather than calling the "It" student's name, the student must pronounce or define the word that student is holding. This is a great rainy day game.

Vocabulary Tic-Tac-Toe!

Choose two topics, such as earthquakes and volcanoes, that your students have studied. Have students choose partners and draw a tic-tac-toe board on a scrap of paper. The first student begins by writing a word in a box that fits one of the categories, such as fault. The partner chooses a word from the other category, such as lava, and writes it in a box. Play continues until one student gets three words from his or her category in a row.

Students can challenge each other's choices and can resolve the challenge by researching the category in a reference book.

Getting Along Together!

Social skills are critical to a child's success in school and in the world at large. Learning those skills early makes success much more likely. Help your students see the benefits of getting along with others and you will set them on the road to maturity.

Have a class discussion in which students develop a list of acceptable and unacceptable behavior. Using the acceptable behavior as a guide, have the class develop a new list of preferred behaviors. Make a Good Citizen chart to post in the classroom listing the preferred behaviors.

> We are going to have to find ways of organizing ourselves cooperatively, sanely, scientifically, harmonically and in regenerative spontaneity with the rest of humanity around earth . . . We are not going to be able to operate our spaceship earth successfully nor for much longer unless we see it as a whole spaceship and our fate as common. It has to be everybody or nobody.
>
> —Buckminster Fuller

Jobs Wanted!

Share the books *Colonial Times From A to Z* (Crabtree Pub., 1998) and *Colonial Crafts* (Crabtree Pub., 1992) by Bobbie Kalman. Discuss how the illustrations show us what life was like for people in colonial times, drawing students attention to the signboards in *Colonial Times From A to Z*.

Talk about different types of jobs with your students. Ask students what jobs are interesting to them. Some students may have already decided what they want to do when they grow up. Others may not have thought about it yet. Tell students they are going to create signs to show what they want to be when they are adults.

Give each student a paper grocery sack to make into a sign. Students slit the sides of the sacks, open them, spread the sacks flat, fold them in half with the printed area on the inside, and glue the two halves together to form a rectangle.

Let students use paint, markers, crayons, and cut-paper decorations to create signs for their career goals. They may need to research symbols that represent the career they chose. Provide encyclopedias and other references for students to use. Or let students create their own free-hand art designs.

Remind students to draw designs on both sides of the sack. Attach strings to the signs. Hang them from the ceiling or from lengths of clothesline hung across the room.

This activity can be used across the curriculum by choosing categories appropriate to the subject. Let your students try some of the following categories.

Category A	Category B
Science vocabulary	Social studies vocabulary
Living characteristics	Non-living characteristics
Words with "ou"	Words with "oi"
Land masses	Oceans
Multiplication facts	Division facts

A Moment of Your Time, Please

Students devise and conduct surveys to discover which are the favorite characters in their sample. Characters could fall into the categories of literary fiction, literary nonfiction, cartoons, television, and movies. Students will have a more varied experience if at least one survey question is open-ended, and one close-ended.

Example of an open-ended question—*Who is your favorite cartoon character?*

Example of an close-ended question—*Which is your favorite movie character? Batman, R2D2 of Star Wars, Matilda, or Judy Jetson?*

There may be a greater range of answers for an open-ended question which students will have to organize.

After they have concluded their sample (at least ten people), they organize their information into a bar graph to present to the class. Discuss and analyze the experience of taking the survey, the kinds of questions that worked best, student opinions about why some questions worked better than others, how the students organized the data, and what would they would do differently the next time. Extend the activity by allowing students to conduct a larger survey of more than one classroom, or of the school. Before doing this, you will check with administrators and teachers whose classes would be surveyed.

> **TIP!**
>
> *Each time you do projects in your classroom, videotape or photograph the presentations and share what was learned with next year's class.*

Resource books

Light in various cultures

Christmas Around the World by Emily Kelley (Carolrhoda, 1986)

Hanukkah: Eight Lights Around the World by Susan Sussman (A. Whitman, 1988)

Seven Candles for Kwanzaa by Andrea Davis Pinkney (Dial BFYR, 1993)

Diwali (Celebrations) by Chris Deshpande (A&C Black, 1998)

Celebrations of Light: A Year of Holidays Around the World by Nancy Luenn (Atheneum, 1998)

Tet: Vietnamese New Year by Dianne M. McMillion (Enslow, 1994)

Purim Play by Roni Schafer (Little, Brown, 1997)

Gung Hay Fat Choy by June Behrens (Children's Press, 1982)

Celebrating Our Differences

Appreciation for diversity among children and cultures should be a part of the daily classroom experience. The realization that we are all different in some ways, yet the same in others needs to be reinforced.

Explore that diversity during the year. One topic you could investigate is the use of light in the customs of many cultures. Begin by reading about Christmas, Hanukkah, Diwali, Kwanzaa, Tet-Trung-Thu, Purim, Chinese New Year, and Noche Buena customs in books. Have students work in small groups. Let each group of students select a culture they would like to learn more about and provide them with a variety of resources to help in the research. Resources might include web sites, library books, or families or community resource people who are willing to be interviewed.

Ask each group to write a report about three customs of the culture they selected. Allow groups to decide how to present what they learned to the class using any of the following presentation ideas: oral or written reports; preparing typical foods; panel discussion; costumes; diorama; poster; mural; creative writing; drama exhibit; music; speaker. Have each group indicate on a map or globe where the culture is located. This activity provides a great

opportunity to get parents and community members involved. Send a note home with each student to locate parents or family friends who have knowledge about different countries or cultures.

TECHNOLOGY

Skills

- Know what is expected of an individual in the world of work: job skills, cooperation, attentiveness, promptness.

- Expand knowledge of relationship between careers and technology.

Industrial Technology Construction Projects

- Plan individual projects.

- Appreciate the use and value of tools and materials. Use tools safely and properly.

- Recognize spatial differences: height, length, width, etc.

- Work with various assembly techniques. Recognize how ordinary resources may be used creatively and economically.

- Use raw materials in a sequential pattern.

- Recognize the relationship between basic hand tools and simple machines: pulley, inclined plane, wheel and axle, wedge, screw, and lever.

> **What we need is imagination. We have to find a new view of the world.**
>
> **—Richard Feynman**

Computer Technology

- Handle the hardware in appropriate ways.

- Develop familiarity with the computer keyboard.

- Use basic software tools and processes appropriately.

- Become familiar with drawing and processing software.

- Use the computer as a research tool.

- Complete assignments using a word processor.

Computer technology curriculum requirements are being written as this book goes to press. Check your school or district for specific curriculum information.

When your students have enough experience with the computer to turn it on and shut it down correctly, demonstrate how to select the application they plan to use and how to get started in it.

Introduce each process slowly so that students do not become lost. If possible, divide the class into small groups and instruct one group at a time. Consult the computer-science instructor or media-technology coordinator in your district for assistance and teaching suggestions. Use a video screen or other group presentation tool if it is available. Ask other third-grade teachers in your district for ideas on how and when to introduce computer skills.

Whether you work in a lab setting or have a computer in your classroom, meet with students before working on the computer and establish a list of rules. Use the following rules as a guide to establishing your own classroom computer rules. Try to keep your rules to five succinct rules.

Have clean hands.

Raise your hand if you have a question.

Touch the keys lightly.

Stay at the same place the instructor is talking about.

Use a quiet voice at all times.

Ask a neighbor for help in a quiet voice if the teacher is busy.

Be careful to touch a key only once at a time.

Use proper keyboarding skills at all times.

If someone says, "Wait," then wait.

The computer can also make doing your work more efficient. Use it to compose parent letters, save them, and reuse them next year. Design other blank letters that can be filled in later. Set up a calendar template for parent communication and organizing. Use the computer to figure grade averages. Store student work on a disk for easy retrieval, rewrites, or absences. Set up a class database that can be used for personalizing mail or creating specific checklists. There are many more uses you will find for the computer as you develop your own records and organization.

VISUAL AND PERFORMING ARTS

Visual Arts Skills

- Name and describe colors, lines, shapes, values, and textures in art and objects in the environments.

- Observe the specific details of design principles such as repetition, rhythm, balance, and variation, in art and in the environment.

- Practice recall of observations.

- Observe that things look different under varying conditions. The conditions to consider are light, color, position, texture, motion, and relative size.

- Demonstrate personal expression and original concepts.

- Incorporate expressive qualities and moods in personal artwork.

- Use a variety of subject matter in personal expression, such as people, animals, plants, places, and events. Images can be based on the environment, from memory, and from the imagination.

- Express the following on two-dimensional surfaces: overlapping of forms; variations in color, size, shape, and texture; repetition of line, shape, and color.

- Use a variety of drawing techniques such as continuous line or action drawing, decorative, imaginative, or realistic styles, and varied effects with the points and sides of crayons, pencils, and chalk.

- Use the following painting techniques: dry and wet brush; stippling; splatter painting; finger painting; color mixing; and crayon-resist washes.

- Model and construct three-dimensional forms with a sense of relative proportion and emphasis, using clay, bread dough, and other materials.

- Apply basic principles of relief printing, including additive (building up a design) and subtractive (carving out a design) methods.

- Use contrasting colors in personal artwork: light and dark; bright and dull; warm and cool.

- Consider all the space in the format.

- Develop crafting abilities with processes such as stitchery, weaving, and papier-mâché.

- Take care of art supplies and materials.

- Recognize similarities and differences among works of art produced at various times and places.

- Tell how art has been used to celebrate personal and historical events.

- Identify how visual arts is used today and how we use art to decorate and enhance daily life.

- Distinguish the art works of specific artists, periods, and cultures.

- Identify aesthetic qualities in visual art work.

- Develop and use art vocabulary.

- Recognize and categorize art forms such as painting, drawing, sculpture, printmaking, and photography.

> **Art flourishes where there is a sense of adventure.**
> —Alfred North Whitehead

Art All Around

Establish an art center in your room. Include the following items: a variety of papers; glue and paste; clay or play dough; art scissors; ribbons and trims; material scraps; buttons; markers; colored pencils; wallpaper scraps; old magazines; paints and brushes; pipe cleaners; plastic foam; straws; and craft sticks.

Provide books or pictures that show the work of well-known painters, such as Vincent Van Gogh, Grandma Moses, Claude Monet, Rembrandt, Georgia O'Keeffe, Pablo Picasso, and Andy Warhol. Show the work of local artists and invite one to visit your class to discuss the artistic process with students. Take field trips to a local art museum or gallery. Allow students to respond by replicating, writing, or discussing feelings about the art work they view. Local high school art instructors can be helpful resources and may provide your class with student assistants.

Windy Art

Have students personalize windsocks to represent their interests or their families. Begin by sharing the history of the windsock. Tell students that windsocks were first used to show pilots the direction of the wind and assist in the safe landing of an aircraft. Now windsocks with brilliant colors hang outside homes as cheerful decorations. In some cultures, the windsock hangs outside when a family is home to welcome visitors. Invite students to bring in windsocks from home to show, and display others to give students ideas.

Give each student a 12" x 18" piece of construction paper of any color. Students decorate the paper flat with colored designs and/or decorations like paper butterfly wings. When the decorations have completely dried, students roll their papers so that the 12-inch ends touch, and staple them together. Punch three holes, equally spaced, around the top edge of the roll and tie an 18-inch length of heavy string in each hole. Tie the three strings together at the top. Glue six 24-inch strips of crepe paper around the bottom of the windsock. Hang the windsocks around the room for everyone to admire. Later let students take them home.

Some useful art reference materials

Come Look With Me Series by Gladys S. Blizzard (Thomasson-Grant Inc.)

Enjoying Art With Children (1990)

Exploring Landscape Art with Children (1992)

Animals in Art (1992)

The World of Art through the eyes of artists Series
by Wendy and Jack Richardson (Children's Press)

Animals (1991)

Cities (1991)

Entertainers (1991)

Families (1991)

The Natural World (1991)

Water (1991)

Portraits of Women Artists for Children Series
by Robyn Montana Turner (Little, Brown and Company, 1992)

Light-Bulb People

Creating 3-D art is an exciting experience. This light-bulb sculpture will become a personal expression for your young artists.

Allow two days for students to plan and complete this activity. Before beginning this project, collect enough light bulbs (new or used) and clean, empty half-pint milk cartons so that each student will have one of each, and you have some extras in case of minor disasters. Remind students be careful, and advise them how to handle clean-up if any bulbs break. Cut the top off the cartons to make a tray about one-inch deep.

Mix plaster of Paris according to the directions on the package and pour plaster into each student's milk tray. Have students insert the screw end of the bulb into the center of the plaster. Tell students that they must work quickly before the plaster hardens and hold the bulbs steady until the plaster is set. Allow them to dry overnight.

Provide glue, ribbons, yarn, material scraps, clay, and markers. Tell students to hold their sculptures by the carton, not the bulb. You may want to have some extra bases with bulbs ready in case of accidents. Students create a "light-bulb person" of their own design. Remind students that three-dimensional art is viewed from all sides. When their creations are complete, have students carefully tear away the milk carton to reveal the sculpture's plaster "pedestal." Display the light-bulb people.

> **A painting [is] a symbol for the universe. Inside it, each piece relates to the other. Each piece is only answerable to the rest of that little world. So, probably in the total universe, there is that kind of total harmony, but we get only little tastes of it.**
>
> **—Corita Kent, Newsweek, December 17, 1984**

Sunset Art

Ask students to watch the sunset for several days and to record the colors and look of the sky in a journal. Discuss shadows and silhouettes. Brainstorm as a class some words that might describe how the sunset makes people feel. Encourage students to write down their feelings.

To help students express those feelings, have them use a 12" x 18" piece of white or light-colored paper. Demonstrate how to use water colors. Use wide brushes to make large sweeping strokes across the paper in the colors they observed in the sunset. Set the paintings aside to dry overnight.

The following day have students cut out silhouettes of objects from black paper to glue on their sunset scenes. Suggest objects such as fences, trees, windmills, flying birds, skyscrapers, or people. Creating their own silhouettes will give children more experience in using perspective, size, and detail in designs. Provide stencils or patterns for students who need or want them. For a striking visual effect, mount the finished paintings on black construction paper to display them.

Sunshine Art

On a very bright, sunny, and calm day let students go outside and make "sunshine" art! Students will need a collection of small objects and a piece of black construction paper. Suggest objects such as buttons, keys, scissors, shoelaces, rocks, or twigs.

Have each student lay the construction paper in direct sunlight and arrange a collection of five to eight items on the paper. Leave the papers in the sun for an hour or two. The length of time depends on how bright the sun is and if it is directly overhead. It is very important that the paper and objects are not moved for the entire exposure time. When the time is up, peek under one item to see if its outline is clearly visible on the paper. Ask students what has created the effect. (The sun bleached the paper around the objects, leaving the "shadow" of each object visible.) If calm sunny days are rare, light-sensitive paper is available at school supply stores, catalogs, and from stores that carry blueprint supplies.

The Sierpinski Triangle

Provide copies of the triangle grid paper on page 62. Choose one triangle on the grid paper at the top of the paper in the center of the grid. Color it. Then, color in the triangle at the bottom left corner of the first colored triangle, and color in the triangle at the bottom right corner of the first colored triangle. Your figure will look like this equilateral triangle with a side length of two triangle units and a blank triangle in the middle. It is your basic figure.

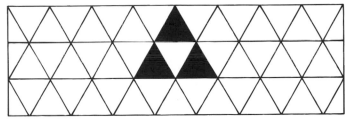

Next, at the bottom left corner of the basic figure, recreate the same triangle, with sides of two units and a blank triangle in the middle. Do the same at the bottom right corner of the basic figure. This is the second figure.

Finally, at the bottom left corner of the second figure, recreate the same triangle, with sides of 4 units and a blank triangle in the middle. Do the same at the bottom right corner of the second figure. Your pattern should now look like this. One large, three medium, and nine small triangles will be shaded. This is the Sierpinski Triangle.

To extend this activity the triangle can be enlarged on posterboard, colored with a variety of colors and patterns. An interesting mural can be created if all student triangles are joined to form one huge Sierpinski Triangle.

Performing Arts Drama Activities

Puppets

Third graders love puppets of all kinds. Even very shy students will come to life as soon as you hand them a puppet. A creative drama center should always include some puppets. Here are some puppets to include in your class drama center.

Stick Puppets: Cut photos out of magazines or catalogs and glue them on clean craft sticks.

Furry Puppets: Purchase stuffed animals at yard sales. Cut them open at the bottom seam and remove the stuffing. Wash the puppets thoroughly, hem the openings (if necessary), and add them to your center.

Finger Puppets: Collect empty film canisters from a photography store and let students glue features and decorations on them to create finger puppets. Colored tape can also be used to create stripes. For example, to make a bumblebee, wrap yellow tape around a black canister, add a black pompon head, black pipe cleaner antennae, and paper wings.

Student Performances

When your students have opportunities to perform at school assemblies, consult them about what they wish to present, within the guidelines outlined by the administration or the Assembly Committee. The enthusiasm level of the class will be much higher if students are allowed to participate in the decision-making process.

59

Music

Skills

- **Listening:** relate scale and chord patterns to a key center or home tone; recognize accented and unaccented beats in sets of twos or threes; recognize the rhythm of the words and the melody of familiar songs when clapped; identify pulse or beat in music written in 6/8 meter; usually two strong pulses or beats to a measure; identify repetition and contrast in songs and recordings; recognize two common designs in music (AB and ABA); differentiate between a major and a minor mode in familiar songs; differentiate between the tonic and dominant chords when accompanying a song; discover the relationship of tempo and dynamics to the text of a song; identify music that gets softer or louder gradually or suddenly; recognize the four families of orchestral instruments by sight and sound.

- **Singing:** sing scale and chord patterns from familiar songs using solfege syllables (do, re, mi, fa, so, la, ti); sing songs in pentatonic (five tones); sing two-part rounds; demonstrate the emotional qualities of the song sung; sing dynamics appropriate to the text of a song.

- **Playing instruments:** play scale patterns, chord patterns, and repeated tones on bells; play longer and more difficult patterns of rhythm on a variety of percussion instruments used by various cultures; play introductions to songs on the autoharp; differentiate between percussion instruments of definite (with) pitch, and those of indefinite (without) pitch; select an appropriate level of dynamics when accompanying singing.

- **Moving:** demonstrate accented and unaccented beats with sets of movements; perform appropriate movements to demonstrate melodic direction.

- **Reading and writing music:** recognize and understand repeat signs; recognize and understand the term *D.C. al Fine* (repeat to the beginning, end at *Fine*); read and note patterns of melody written in staff notation using

> My message to the world is "Let's swing, sing, shout, make noise! Let's not mimic death before our time comes! Let's be wet and noisy."
>
> —Mel Brooks, interview, <u>New York Times</u>, March 30, 1975

manipulatives (staff boards and magnetic or flannel boards).

- **Creating:** improvise more complex melodies and rhythmic patterns, using appropriate sound sources; create introductions and codas to familiar songs, using tonal instruments; create phrasewise movements to songs from several cultures.

- Explore the qualities of sound (both vocal and instrumental) that are expressive of the student's own as well as different cultures.

- Begin to compare music of the present with music of the past.

Mood Music

Tape a long sheet of butcher paper across the chalkboard. Play a short classical music selection. As the class watches, use two crayons to make line drawings that illustrate the way you are feeling as you listen. When the beat is faster, make the lines jump up and down quickly. When the beat slows, make the lines thicker and more deliberate. When tones are high, make the crayon marks wispy; as bass notes are introduced, make deep, dark images.

While students listen quietly to a different piece of classical music, ask them to think about how they feel when they hear those notes. Let each student select two crayons that represent those feelings. Have students make line drawings on a large sheet of paper as the music plays again.

Extend the activity by using colors to represent different instruments in the orchestra, such as yellow for the brass section, blue for the woodwinds, red for the percussion, and green for the string section.

Liquid and Lyrics

Give small groups of students five clear glasses and tell them they are going to create music using five different notes. Many students may have already experimented with various water levels to create the scale and will repeat that effort here. To extend the activity, encourage groups to brainstorm other things that could be used in the glasses and see what results they have. Provide gelatin, sand, pebbles, sugar, or marbles for students to experiment with. When they are ready, have each group play a tune for the class.

Crazy Compositions

Many of your students may be familiar with "Weird Al" Yankovic and his song adaptations. His work is amusing and can be found on the Internet using *Weird Al* as keywords. Have students suggest songs from camp, nursery rhymes, or family favorites. Group four or five students together and have them select a song they all know. Tell the groups to rewrite their songs using a subject they are learning in school.

Write the following examples on the board. Sing them through as a class. Leave them on the board for groups to refer to during the activity.

Water Cycle
(Tune: My Darling Clementine)

Evaporation, condensation, precipitation,
it is true,

Are called the water cycle and
it's never really through.

Food Chain
(Tune: The Foot Bone's Connected to the Ankle Bone)

The grain seed is eaten by the ground squirrel.
The ground squirrel's eaten by the rattlesnake.
The rattlesnake's eaten by the cougar.
Now that's the food chain.

Easy-to-make Musical Instruments
Coffee Can Drums

Collect coffee or other cans without a top. Cut off the top of a balloon and stretch it across the top of the can. Secure with a rubber band around the rim. To play the drum students can use a pencil or their hands to beat the tops of the drums, rub pencils up and down the sides of the cans, or tap the metal bottoms of the cans.

Maracas

Take two yogurt or pudding cups. Place 10-20 dried beans or small pebbles in one of the cups and glue the openings of the cups together. Allow to dry. Reinforce the glue by taping the cups together with masking tape at the seam. Glue white paper to the outside of the cups to make surfaces that can be decorated, or glue decorative wrapping paper around the cups. Add decorations if desired. Shake the maracas to make musical sounds.

Tambourine

Have each student decorate the bottoms of two paper plates. Staple the plates almost completely together along the outside rims of the plates, decorated sides out. Put a handful of beans inside the plates and finish stapling.

Rain Stick

Use the cardboard core from a roll of paper towels and close one end with tape and paper. Twist a small coat hanger so that it fits inside. Add a handful of rice or beans. Close the open end with tape and paper. Cover the entire paper towel roll with brown paper from a paper bag reinforcing the closures at the end. Decorate the rain stick to look like wood. You may find pliers or a wire cutter helpful for working with the hanger.

61

Triangle Grid Paper

ACTIVITIES FOR A THEMATIC UNIT CALLED CHANGE

Thematic units should integrate learning skills across the curriculum. They can be developed as a focused unit or encompass mini-units or sections like links in a large chain. For example, the thematic unit called Change planned on page 14 includes a series of sections concerning changing seasons, growth and development of plants and animals, community changes, and a light-hearted section using cookies.

The thematic unit section on cookies can be kicked off by reading *The Great Chocolate Chip Cookie Contest* by Barbara Douglass (Lothrop, 1985). It is the story of a class that decides to have a contest to see which student can make the best chocolate chip cookie. Allow at least two weeks to complete this section. Fill your room with books about cookies and bakeries, and cookbooks for students to look through during the unit. Search the Internet for the home pages of companies like Hershey and Nestle, or call the toll-free numbers listed on their products to obtain teaching kits available from these corporations. March is National Chocolate Chip Cookie Month—the perfect time for this section of a unit on change.

Check whether your school has cooking facilities available to teachers. If facilities on campus are available, decide if you want everyone to bake on the same day or one group each day for the week. If everyone bakes together, bring in volunteer help. If some bake each day, arrange for freezer space. If there are no facilities available on campus, you could have students mix the dough which you take home to bake, or have students bake at home and bring in the results.

Language Arts

Read *The Great Chocolate Chip Cookie Contest* to your class. Discuss the story and tell students they will have a contest like the one in the story. As a class, plan how to set up and begin the contest.

Other language arts projects include writing poems or songs about chocolate chip cookies, compiling a class cookbook, videotaping and editing the contest, writing fantasy stories about chocolate chips, and researching and writing reports about chocolate and how chocolate chips are made.

Math

Ask students to bring copies of their favorite cookie recipes to school to compare the ingredients. Divide students into teams of two or three and have each team decide which recipe to use. Have students use the recipe to create a grocery list. Arrange a class trip to a grocery store or ask students to make the trip with parents to price the ingredients and determine what it will cost to make the cookies.

When each team has selected its recipe, meet with each team to review baking vocabulary and ingredient amounts. Challenge students to adjust the ingredient amounts to make a half-batch or a double batch.

Science and Math

Arrange centers that include a collection of baking utensils for students to identify. Use baking vocabulary as the spelling list. One center might offer a variety of candy chips—colored, chocolate, white, oversized, or mini—for students to examine. Have students compare, weigh, and measure the chips. Remind students not to eat these chips because they are not clean.

Discuss with your students the ingredients that cause chemical changes in the cookies, such as baking soda. Invite a home economist or extension agent to visit your class to show why accurate measuring is essential to maintain good results. If time permits, show students what happens if you put too much flour in a cookie (tough texture) or forget the baking soda (cookie will not rise).

There are many opportunities in this unit to follow scientific processes of questioning, hypothesizing, testing, observing, and concluding.

Let students theorize about which of two types of chocolate chips might melt first. Ask students to form a hypothesis and discuss how to test it. Supervise them as they observe and time the chips as they melt. Have students conclude what happened and record the results. Now ask students to observe the reverse process and see which of the two chocolate chips hardens faster.

Social Studies

Field Trip—Tour a local bakery or cookie shop, or ask the owner to visit your class and describe what work goes on in a bakery. Make a class list of questions ahead of time.

Geography—Have a chocolate chip cookie for each student. Place each cookie on a piece of blue construction paper so that the cookie looks like an island surrounded by water. Ask students to look closely at the cookie, and identify any "land forms" they see. Tell students to look for mountains, plains, cliffs, valleys, or rock formations. Provide magnifying glasses for students to look through. Encourage students to use their imaginations.

Ask the following questions: *Does anyone see a crater? Why is it there? Does anyone have a cookie with a harbor area? or dried-up riverbeds?*

Have students list the land forms they find and compare their findings with classmates.

Ask students to measure the island and create a realistic scale that tells how large it might be if it were really an island. *(Example: 1 inch = 100 miles)* Have them make maps of their cookie island. Then let students eat the cookie.

Ask a parent volunteer to provide homemade cookies if your schedule doesn't permit baking time. (Homemade cookies are best because they have more variety of texture and are more likely to be irregular in shape.)

To extend the lesson, ask students to write a story about an adventure they had on their cookie islands using the words from the landforms list they created.

Economics—Encourage each team to figure out how to raise money to pay for the ingredients. Possible funding sources are parents who would be willing to donate the items needed, the PTA, and students earning the money by collecting aluminum cans. If someone is willing to loan students the cost of the ingredients, the class could hold a bake sale at the end of the project and sell individually wrapped cookies to other classes to repay the loan. Real-life lessons in business will result as techniques of advertising, bookkeeping, marketing, and pricing are used. Check your school's rules regarding the sale of home-baked items. If your school allows the sale of only commercially prepared items, use the money students earn to buy different brands of commercially produced cookies.

Group Goal Setting—Have all students work together to design, submit, and accept a cookie judging sheet. This way all students are aware ahead of time what will be expected and how the process will be conducted. Encourage them to express fairness concerns before the final criteria are accepted.

Culminating Activity—Invite the principal or ask a local baker to your class to judge the cookie contest. Prizes could be awarded such as certificates, ribbons, or colorful pencils. You may want to establish enough award categories so that every group "wins." Some categories to choose from are Best-Shaped Cookie, Most Chips, Tastiest, Prettiest Brown Color, Crunchiest, Softest, Least Crumbly, and the Best All-Around!

> **Winning is overemphasized. The only time it is really important is in surgery and war.**
>
> **—Al McGuire**

Wrap-Up

As you complete these activities, talk about how a great cookie depends upon all of the ingredients being blended together well, and the importance of following the directions in order to create a quality product. Stress that every cookie will not be the same shape or have an equal numbers of chips. Tell students that they are just like those cookies! Everyone in the class is a different and unique individual, but by working together and appreciating each other's strengths they were able to create something that everyone could enjoy.

A Little Extra

Try this class chant for a quick fill in!

Leader: Who stole the cookies from the cookie jar?
Class: Sam stole the cookies from the cookie jar.
Sam: Who me?
Class: Yes, you!
Sam: Couldn't be!
Class: Then, who?
Sam: Joe stole the cookies from the cookie jar.

Continue until all students have had a turn.

CHAPTER THREE: THE CLASSROOM

LAYOUT OF THE CLASSROOM

Logistics

Before you start rearranging classroom furniture, do it on paper first to see if it works. This will save you time and save your back!

Use graph paper to draw your room to scale. Cut out pieces of paper to represent the large items. Be sure these items are to scale as well. Now manipulate the pieces until you have a comfortable working plan.

Here are some things to keep in mind as you arrange your classroom.

- Keep the art center close to a water source.

- Keep the display areas at a third grader's eye level.

- Label everything or let your students label items so that clean up is child-centered.

- Remember you will need center areas, individual work areas, small group areas, and a large group area.

- Try arranging areas for multiple uses. Can individual desks be grouped for small group work? Can centers also be used as individual work stations?

- Use the floor plan on the facing page to help you.

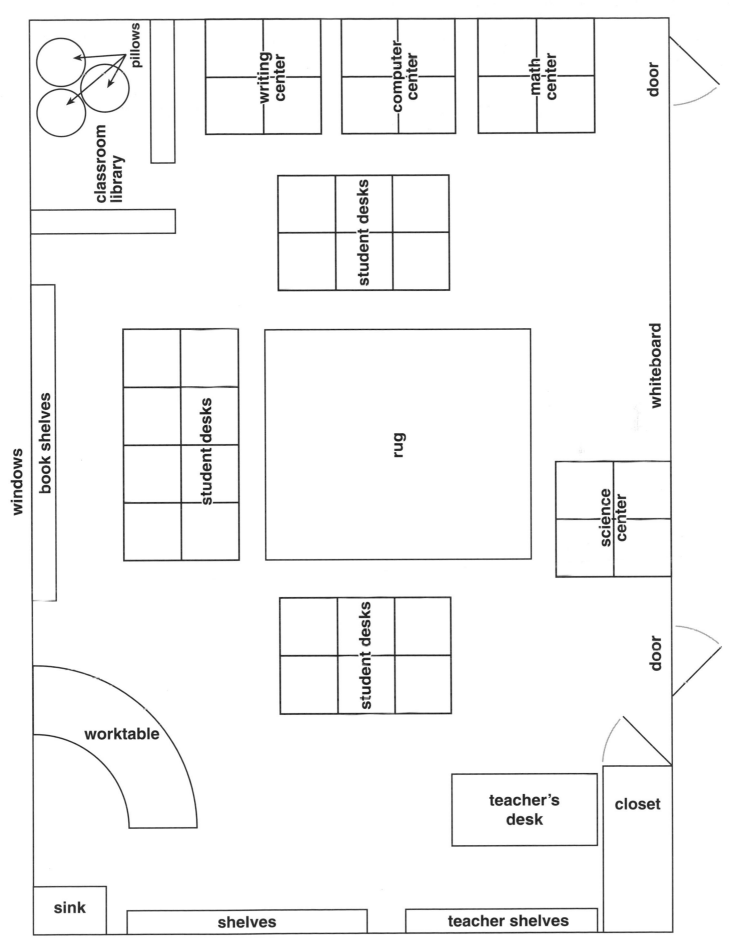

Daily Schedule
8:00 - 3:00

8:00 Entry Task/Special Project

8:40 Opening and Community Time

9:00 Math

9:45 Recess

10:05 Reading/Writing Workshop

11:30 Lunch and Recess

12:15 Shared Oral Reading

12:35 Science or Social Studies

1:20 M, W PE
T, Th Visual Arts
F Extended Lab

2:05 M, W Music
T, TH Visual Arts, cont.
F Extended Lab, cont.

2:45 Closing

3:00 Dismissal

SCHEDULING

Following a daily schedule will make you more effective as a teacher. Schedules let the students know what is coming next, and keep you on track. To make a schedule, start by finding out what times may be planned for you already. Your school may have music, art, or science programs that regularly require students to be away from your classroom. Your principal may want to have all students who are in an English Language Development Program to be meeting at the same time. There are usually scheduled recess or lunch times. Once you know when students will be with you, divide the day into blocks of time for each subject. Opportunities to read, write, and work with mathematics should occur every day. Your school or district may have requirements about the minimal amount of time that should be devoted to certain subjects.

Many teachers write their schedule on a posterboard and post it in the class. Other prefer to write it on the board so that students get in the habit of consulting it every day. If it is written on a chalkboard or easel pad every day, writing it can become a student job. Third graders love to write "official" signs. They are proud to create something for the class.

> **My idea of education is to unsettle the minds of the young and inflame their intellects.**
>
> **—Robert Hutchins**

The Entry Task or Special Project

Start the day with an entry task or a special project. Post a different task on the chalkboard or an easel every day. Suggested entry tasks are journal entries in science, writing, personal, or math journals, or Sustained Silent Reading (see description of SSR on page 21). When students arrive, they check the task notice. This allows students some time to make the transition from home, morning care, or school bus to class. Frequently students arrive at school having been rushed every moment since they woke up. With an entry task, they can put their things away, get out what they need for the entry task, and get to work at their own pace. The entry task helps students settle and focus, and gives you time for last-minute preparations or to handle any last minute crisis.

Scheduling a regular special project time early in the day gives you a lot of flexibility for doing many projects. You and your students will enjoy having a block of time to work on long- or medium-term cross-curricular projects at a time of day when the students are generally able to concentrate easily. Special projects could include developing a board game, preparing a class magazine, writing and rehearsing a play, building props for a class production, and so on.

The Opening and Community Time

Possible activities for the opening of the day include the flag salute, taking attendance, checking-in homework, a community meeting, introducing theme activities, and a presentation of activities planned for the day. Establish a routine for the Opening. The Opening can set the tone for the day. Interact and observe your students as you go through the activities. You will quickly learn to spot who is having a hard day and may need some encouragement to get on track.

Closing

Use the last fifteen minutes of the day to bring your class back together for a group activity. You can use this time to summarize the day with a closing activity like the Activity Review Cards described below, review the homework assignment for the evening, remind students of any special events of the next day, or to pass out special recognitions you would like to give. Your students will benefit by having a few moments of mental regrouping before they have to go home, go to day car, or get on a bus. You will benefit by taking an opportunity to assess the instructional day with your students and having a relatively calm end of the day.

Activity Review Cards

As part of your closing activities, review the lessons and activities of the day as a group. Appoint one student to date and write on a 5" x 7" card as the other students summarize the day's activities. Display the index cards, adding to the display for the month. At the end of the month bind the cards into a class book for the classroom library, and prepare for the next month's activity review. You will all enjoy rereading the activity books at different points in the year. An additional benefit is that you will have an instant assessment of what parts of your instructional day were most effective.

CLASSROOM CENTERS

Centers are extremely beneficial in any classroom to extend a topic, master a skill, provide for learning differences, and to stimulate creative thinking. There are many space-sensitive centers that can be arranged without overwhelming your classroom.

TIP!

If classroom ceilings are low, purchase a plant pole and position it in a corner. Hang bags on the hooks with clothespins or hang them from hangers on the plant pole.

Organizing Centers

Laminate worksheets that enrich curriculum. Let students work them using water-based pens. Keep a supply of clean-up wipes handy. Worksheets can be filed in large manila envelopes by topic. An alternative to laminating is to slip the worksheets in plastic three-ring notebook sleeves. Identify the worksheets as math, science, etc., and use indexes to indicate the skills.

Place manipulatives such as place value blocks, tangrams, and letter blocks in plastic zipper bags. Label the bags using self-stick labels or permanent markers. Store the bags in a plastic tub or punch holes just under the closure and hang them on hooks from a pegboard. Magnetic hooks can be placed on a file cabinet, whiteboard, or the back of a metal desk to provide convenient sites to hang bags.

Sample Center Ticket

Joshua's Center Ticket
Date
Center
What I Did Today

Sept. 16
Reading
Read Cloudy With a Chance of Meatballs

Sept. 17
Science
Made a thermometer model

Sept. 18
Math and Social Studies
Built a shelter with place value blocks.

Sept. 19
Made rain painting

Sept. 20
Free Choice
Wrote a poem about meatball weather.

Records of Center Use

Prepare each center with clothespins either hanging from a short clothesline or clipped onto a board. Control the number of students at each center by limiting the number of clothespins available.

Give each student a "Center Ticket." The center ticket has the student's name and lists all centers on it. When students arrive in the morning, they choose the centers they want to visit that day and clip their tickets to one of the clothespins at those centers. At center time the student completes the activities at the center, writes the date on the center ticket and writes a quick reflection on what he or she accomplished. The next day the student hangs the center ticket at a different center. Once a center is marked the student cannot return to that center until his or her center ticket is completely filled. See the sample center ticket in the sidebar for reference.

For your records, at the beginning of each week, prepare a class roster with a list of centers available that week and any special activities at them. Update your center tracking sheet on a regular basis by reviewing center tickets and checking off student activities. This task can be undertaken by students as part of their classroom responsibilities.

CLASSROOM LIBRARY

Classify your classroom library using a system that your students can manage independently. Code your books by level or topic using colored self-adhesive dots. Cut boxes diagonally low in front and high in back to create book files. Cover them with colorful self-adhesive paper which you could color coordinate with the dots. For example you could put a blue dot on all the books about space and a blue dot on the space book box, or put a green dot on all the environmental science books and green paper around the environmental science book files. Reshelving books is easy with color-coding. Assign students to be classroom librarians.

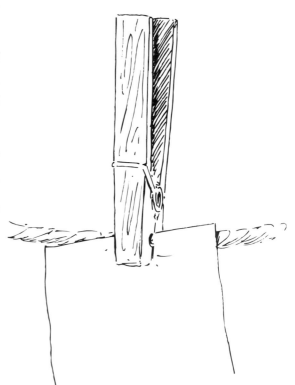

ORGANIZING YOUR TEACHING ARCHIVES

If you do a little planning before you start, you'll be surprised at how easy it is to stay organized!

Establish a file box for each unit. Label the outside and place a file or notebook inside it to record and organize your teaching ideas. Keep an index of units in a three-ring notebook as a master to track your ideas at a glance. You can also use it as a place for writing great ideas you hear, print from the Internet, or copy from other resources. Record which activities worked well and indicate changes you want to make for next year. If you use a plan book, update it as well with comments. As you plan for a unit, get out the three-ring notebook, the unit box, and last year's plan book (when you have one!) and sort through the ideas.

You can also create an overview of teaching ideas on your computer. Using a spreadsheet, establish fields such as unit, core literature, writing activity, integration activity, cooking project, art project, and curriculum correlation. Fill in an activity for each cell and you can quickly document for administrators that you are covering curriculum topics.

Storage Ideas

Much of the packaging that surrounds or tops our food can be reused in the classroom as manipulatives, art supplies, or storage containers to provide you with low or no cost materials.

Use appropriately sized boxes at centers for pencils and other equipment that may be needed at the center. At the art center fill several with colored pencils, marker sets, fancy-cut scissors, foil scraps, and other materials.

Outfit boxes with project supplies for easy transportation from one location to another. Fill them with pencils, crayons, a glue stick, and scissors. This will eliminate lots of return trips for supplies.

When a large group art project requires many tiny pieces, give each student a box with the required items. It will speed up your art time considerably and keep things neat and organized!

Sets of manipulatives stay together when you store the tiny cubes or chips in boxes.

Fill boxes with milk tops or other counters so students will have easy access to counters they can sort by color, use as bingo markers, or use to practice patterning skills.

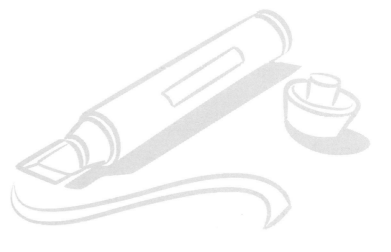

Teaching is a moral calling, a craft, and an intellectual occupation. It is often values that bring one to education in the first place. The craft develops through experience and reflection upon that experience. What is hardest to maintain in the midst of the immediate demands of the classroom is the intellectual aspect of teaching, which, though less apparent on an everyday level than the craft issues, still pervades and underlies every good teacher's practice. It has to do with teachers' analysis of how children learn, of the role of ethnicity, gender, and class in learning, of the relationship between school and society, and of the translation of moral values into specific classroom practice.

—Herbert Kohl

> **Before beginning, prepare carefully.**
>
> —Cicero

RECORDKEEPING

One of the keys to a successful classroom is being organized. Know what records your school requires, and what records your teaching plans require. Records you may need to keep include daily attendance records, assessment records (including portfolios and test results), lesson plans, permanent school records (usually kept at the school), homework tracking, and reading logs. Plan your recordkeeping as soon as you know you have a class. Good recordkeeping should not significantly add to your workload. Search for a method that is convenient and does not need to be recopied or duplicated in another location.

Daily Attendance

An attendance record book is extremely useful. Its obvious purpose is keeping track of attendance, but it has other uses as well. Update this book every day, and keep it close to the classroom exit where it is easy to grab in an emergency. In the event of a fire, earthquake, or other disaster, you need to be able to call roll and check and see that each student is accounted for. If something has happened to prevent you from calling roll, the person in charge of your class will need the information.

Even if your school or district provides computerized attendance sheets, keeping personal records is extremely useful for parent conferences and tracking patterns of absences that may be red flags to other problems the student is facing or help explain poor performance in the class.

Grade Book

You will need a grade book. List students' names in alphabetical order. If you have space on the page, leave some blank lines between student names so that you can add new students in alphabetical order when they join your class. Assign different pages in the grade book to different subjects. Ask for a copy of the report card you must fill out for each student, so that you know what information you must record and report. You will be using different assessment criteria for different types of work. Label sections for homework, projects and reports, and tests.

Record grades daily or weekly. Try to keep the paper flowing through your room so you don't drown in it. As you record grades, include information on the grade book that will help you identify the source of the grade when it comes time to do progress reports. For example, in the spelling section you might note at the top of a column of test results, the date of the test and the total number of questions or words included on the test. In a social studies section you might note the name of the project graded and include a column for a content grade, a column for the mechanics grade, and an overall grade.

Record Sheets

Make a record sheet where you can track who is turning in homework on time. You may need similar sheets for your computer center and other centers. Each week put out a new sheet and review and file the previous week's records.

Anecdotal Records

Card Method

Lay a file folder flat on the table. Write each student's name at the bottom of a 4" x 6" index card. Place the cards on the file folder, covering the folder. Make sure that the student's name on each index card is completely visible, then staple each card to the file folder. Now you can leave the file folder on your desk and jot anecdotal records of your observations on each student's card.

When a card becomes full, remove and file it, then add a new card to the folder. You may want to make several color-coded cards for each child— using a blue card for observations during reading time, or a pink card for notes about the student's writing.

Label Method

Create a file folder for each student. Clip a number of sheets of self-adhesive labels to a clipboard. As you observe a student, write the student's name and the date on one of the labels and make your note. At the end of the day, transfer the labels into the file folders you have made for each student. If you have access to a computer and computer labels, print student names on labels before using them.

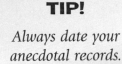

TIP!

*Always date your
anecdotal records.*

Permanent Records

Most schools and districts have a permanent record that is maintained for each student throughout the child's school experience. Check with your principal or other teachers about what information you are required to complete for each student.

This document is used as a reference by future teachers of the student and other school personnel. It can also be consulted by parents. It is generally a good idea to word any information written in this document with a positive or a neutral tone, and to avoid irrelevant opinions.

ASSESSMENT

There are several important steps to successfully communicating a student's progress to the administration and the child's parents. First, know what you want to assess. This is information you'll develop in your planning, know from reviewing the curriculum you are to teach, and from reviewing the report card before you set up your assessment system. Next, design an assessment system and gather or know the assessment tools you will use, such as anecdotal records, teacher-made and other tests, student evaluations, rubrics, and portfolio review (see below). Third, evaluate the assessment data. Finally, communicate the information about the student's progress.

Below are some ideas to help you assess each student's work, knowledge, and progress.

Portfolios

A portfolio is a collection of a student's work in each subject area that reflects the student's abilities. Keep both formal and informal portfolios for each student. Involve your students in selecting work to be kept in these files. Portfolios are the most useful tool for recognizing conceptual growth and for seeing the changes that the student is making throughout the school year.

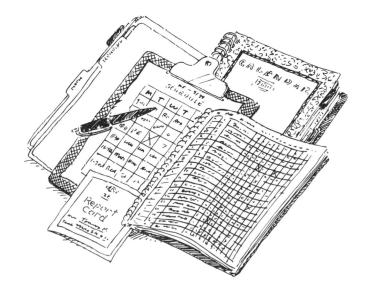

Rubric for a Newspaper Advertisement

4= Excellent
Language: Exciting variety of word images

Ideas: New, original ideas

Focus: Stays on topic

Mechanics: Very few errors

3= Good Job
Language: Some variety of word images

Ideas: A new approach or idea

Focus: Includes some details on the topic

Mechanics: Some errors

2= Meets goals
Language: Commonly-found word images

Ideas: Heard it before

Focus: Not focused on topic

Mechanics: Many errors

1= Not yet
Language: Repeated words

Ideas: Incomplete ideas

Focus: Didn't know what the topic was

Mechanics: Multiple errors that should have been corrected

Rubrics

A rubric is an assessment method that outlines evaluation criteria for each project. The advantage of a rubric is that everyone knows the expectations prior to completing the assignment. Create the rubric alone or ask students for their input and create one as a class. Look at the example in the sidebar. Before an assignment to write the newspaper ad, students discuss and decide the evaluation standards for an excellent ad, good ad, an acceptable ad, and a poor ad.

Allow students to do peer assessments with rubrics and then conference with the author. You can also design more categories for a rubric if an assignment is complex and the characteristics of what is acceptable need to be described with more detail.

Report Cards

As you figure grades for report cards, you will probably be able to use your best judgment about what work should be reflected in the final grade and what can be given greater or lesser importance. Before you sit down to write your report cards, gather all relevant material— portfolios, your grade book, and anecdotal records. Expect to spend a week or two doing report cards. Some schools and districts provide pre-printed report card forms that you fill in. Others will provide you with blank forms on which to hand write grades that become the permanent report card. It can be useful to make copies of your blank forms—one for each student. You can compile your records on this sheet, and so that any mistakes you make (and you will make some) will be on a nonpermanent record. When finished, copy the grades onto the permanent report card.

What are the important grades to include in this reporting period? Some schools and districts will mandate some reporting. Others will leave it to your professional judgment. Is every grade as important as the others?

Some teachers like to drop the worst grade from the student's work and then average the rest of the grades. Others like to weight different work differently.

Example of Weighting Grades

For example, Johanna, the third-grade teacher, needs to calculate a science grade for Lita Brown. The assignments and grades she has recorded for Lita are the following.

In-class project
raising and observing a plant
Total possible points—5
Grade—5 or 100%

Homework assignment
gathering different seeds and comparing them
Total possible points—4
Grade—4 or 100%

Keeping a discovery journal
Lita wrote in the journal extensively every day.

Two in-class science tests
Grade—7/10 (7 correct of 10) or 70%
Grade—6/9 (6 correct of 9) or 67%

You can see that Lita's exploration and discovery work is excellent as reflected in the grades. She doesn't do as well on tests.

Lita participates actively in class.

Johanna could decide that the discovery and exploration aspects of the curriculum are worth 75% of the grade, tests will be worth 15%, and class participation, 10%.

She will figure Lita's grade by adding the exploration and discovery aspects together. She then averages the grade by dividing the total by the number of items included in the total.

Plant project	100
Seed homework	100
Journal	100
Total is	300/3 = 100%

Since 75 is the value for exploration and discovery, then 100% of 75 = 75 (or 75 x 1.0). As she has 100% in the discovery part of the grade, she will receive the full 75 points of the grade.

Test 1	70%
Test 2	67%
Total is	137%/2 = 69%

Since 15 is the value for tests, then 69% of 15 = 10 (15 x .69). She would receive 10 points of a possible 15 for her tests.

She participates actively in class, so Johanna will give her the full 10 points for class participation.

Lita's total grade is therefore 75 + 10 + 10 = 95.

You can weight your grading system to reflect your curricular goals. Once you have made a decision, treat all students the same way. Make a note of your grade formula for future reference.

Student achievement can be interpreted only in light of the quality of the program they experience.
—National Science Education Standards

Report Card Comments

Many report cards have sections for teacher comments. Draft your comments on a separate sheet of paper before you write them on the final document. Edit your comments for content and mechanical errors. Use a positive tone when writing report cards. Your words will be remembered for many years.

To make it a bit easier, try some of these phrases to help you describe your third graders. Add a few comments of your own to personalize them! If a student has done an exceptional project or shows excellence in any academic, recreational, or social area, mention it specifically.

—shows interest in improving in _____.

—is willing to stick with the job until it is done correctly.

—performs well on tasks that he or she has chosen to do.

—is considerate of others.

—responds well to correction.

—is becoming more dependable.

—listens well in _____ class.

—is sacrificing speed for accuracy.

—is learning to be a better listener.

—is continuing to grow in independence.

—working on thinking before writing.

—is learning to participate in group activities.

—is well-adjusted.

—seeks information when confused.

—uses more than one strategy to solve a problem.

—made steady progress in _____.

—shows growth in _____.

—is reluctant to contribute.

CHAPTER FOUR: RELATIONSHIPS

RELATIONSHIPS WITH YOUR STUDENTS

Treat each student as an individual.

Treat each student with respect.

Spend time every day listening to each student.

Challenge each student to risk and try new things.

Set high expectations for all.

Provide the support that students need to learn.

Follow the same rules you expect class members to follow.

Demonstrate your good sense of humor, especially when things don't go well.

Be realistic about what you and your class can accomplish.

Be consistent with discipline and goals.

Be willing to say, "I don't know, but we'll find out."

Separate minor issues from major ones.

Celebrate diversity.

Rejoice with the class when goals are reached.

Believe that everyone learns by making mistakes and demonstrate it.

Practice what you preach.

Communicate Personal Goals

Outline your personal goals as a teacher to your students. Use the list found on page 76 or one you have written. Show them what you are striving for and what you believe in.

Student Conflict

Third graders have a strong sense of fairness that usually stems from their personal point of view. The climate of your classroom will be conducive to learning if you can create and maintain an air of justice, equality, and fairness.

Involve students in establishing the rules for the class. At the beginning of the year, have an open discussion of what rules students think are fair and reasonable for the class to abide by. As they contribute, record the ideas and then combine, clarify, or restate the rules until everyone understands them. You may find that your class wants to have a lot of rules, some that pertain to minutia. You may wish to suggest to students that they keep their rules to about five in number and avoid repeating currently existing school rules. At the same time rules are being set, have students decide consequences for not following the rules. Consequences should be reasonable and reflect the philosophy of your school or district.

Record the final draft on chart paper and place it in a prominent place in the classroom. Statements should be positively stated: "Walk in our room" rather than "Don't run." Students should sign their names to the compact—use a feather pen and fancy calligraphy for fun! Make desk-size copies for notebooks and send a copy home to parents.

Third graders may be new to conflict resolution, so begin by modeling the expected behavior. Ask another staff member, an older student, or a student to role play a scene with you. Show students how to state the problem, express how they feel about the problem, offer a solution, and then compromise with others.

> **We have one simple rule here: Be kind.**
>
> —Sam Jaffe, <u>Lost Horizon</u>, 1937

If the entire class is struggling with one of the rules, call a class meeting to discuss the infraction. At the first meeting you may need to model for students how to disagree with courtesy, how to accept the class's decision, and how to think independently.

If two students are involved in a conflict, guide them to solve the problem together. Find a quiet place where they can discuss the issue without interruption or input from others. A small bench or two chairs facing each other in a "Peacemaking Corner" will work. Excuse yourself, but stay within hearing distance in case you are needed. You may need to give the pair a five-minute time limit to reach a solution without mediation. If that is impossible, you or a peer may need to assist the students in reaching a solution.

Predictable Student Problems

As sure as the sun will rise in the east, third graders will present you with similar behavioral and relationship problems every year. How you deal with these predicaments, however, should not be predictable. You will have to evaluate the solutions and consequences based on the reactions and responses of the individual student. Always communicate to the student the feeling and the words that indicate that you know this behavior can improve. Below are some typical student problems followed by suggestions for dealing with them.

"Sam is too shy!"

Help the student make a list of things that he or she is comfortable doing. When projects require expertise in that area, encourage Sam to lead the way! Try pairing two shy students together so that one of them has to take a leadership role. Shy students are sensitive, so be aware of their sensibilities when you discuss their work and ways to improve it.

"Jo(e) is too aggressive!"

Help this student make a list of things that good friends do, such as share, take turns, or let someone else talk. Suggest Jo(e) pick one of those traits to focus on for the day. Later, let him or her tell you or another adult how the day went.

"Aaron/Erin is a bully!"

Role-play some bullying scenarios in the classroom without finger-pointing at Aaron/Erin. This will help the class learn to deal with a bully. Later talk with the bully about the behavior. If necessary, point out a recent event that exhibited the bullying. Make it clear you have zero tolerance for bullying behavior. When you see a bully using acceptable behavior, let the student know you've noticed.

If a bully is picking on one particular student, you may need to establish a silent signal so that the victim can indicate when he or she needs help. A lot of growth may need to occur before the bully and the victim can confront one another. Be patient and include parents in the solution.

"Eli/Ellie is excluded!"

This scenario is a daily routine in third-grade classrooms. The student who is excluded may be different every day, but the process is the same. Every day someone has a new "best friend" and ignores yesterday's "best friend." This is especially true among third-grade girls. You can try to help by saying, "I see this group needs another helper," or "Eli/Ellie is ready to help you!" to guide the student into the group.

If the exclusion persists and the same student is left out of the group every day, take action early. Gather the students in the excluding group together while Eli/Ellie is occupied helping in the library or assisting a teacher. Discuss why they are excluding Eli/Ellie and the hurtful nature of their actions. See if the students in the group can suggest a solution, but be ready to suggest the next action. Privately conference with Ellie/Eli to be sure he or she understands how to react. Stress the positive events that have occurred and encourage him or her to become involved. Again parents can be a major asset in resolving this situation.

> **This is what knowledge really is. It is finding out something for oneself with pain, with joy, with exultancy, with labor, and with all the little ticking, breathing moments of our lives, until it is ours as that only is ours which is rooted in the structure of our lives.**
>
> —Thomas Wolfe, <u>The Web and the Rock</u>, 1939

Student Social Order

Right from the start, initiate the idea that your classroom is a community.

Have students arrange some or all of the furniture and put up labels and signs that they have made. The more student participation and choice you are willing to incorporate in your room, the more responsibility students will take for the operation of the room.

Students should assume responsibilities for as many tasks as feasible. You will be amazed at the level of independence and reliability you will witness as you allow them to be in charge.

Provide students with many opportunities to choose their activities during the day, such as which centers to use, what to read, how to respond to literature, which topics to study, creative problem solving, and groupings. Having choices helps make students content and cooperative, which you will appreciate, and they learn how to choose well.

Let students know you expect them to respect others, themselves, authority, and property. Modeling this respect for each of them will demonstrate your expectations.

Celebrate the diversity of the class. Discuss cultural heritages, invite families to share ethnic cooking, speak positively of the contributions of various cultures, and share ethnic customs.

Let students experience your pride in their accomplishments. Rejoice with them as their best efforts pay off. Display their creations, publish their writing, and communicate your excitement to their families.

ADMINISTRATORS

Your administrator can be your best ally or your worst enemy! Because you need to be allies, attempt to establish a positive relationship from the start. Make a list of any questions that occur to you regarding school policy and procedures. That way you can schedule a single meeting to obtain answers to many concerns. Your administrator will appreciate your efficiency.

If you disagree with a procedure, calmly state your viewpoint and offer a viable alternative. Clearly and concisely express your reasoning.

If your suggestion is turned down or you find yourself forced to follow a procedure you disagree with, conduct yourself as a professional. You can look for another opportunity to revise the rules at a later time.

Attend all faculty meetings. Be prompt and participate in discussions. Listen to others and request information on previous methods before becoming too vocal.

When you see positive things happening around the school, mention them to the administrator.

When the administrator visits your room, introduce him or her to the class. Include him or her in an activity. Encourage students to show their work to the administrator during the visit and outside of the classroom. Invite your administrator to help with a special project or to become a regular participant in "math facts" practice once a week.

> **Taking an interest in what students are thinking and doing is often a much more powerful form of encouragement than praise.**
>
> —Robert Martin

SCHOOL STAFF

Create a "School Staff" bulletin board in your classroom. Provide a camera to your students and have them take photos of staff members, such as the principal, secretary. cafeteria staff, librarian, paraprofessionals, counselors, nurse, the custodian, and all the others. Have students mount the photos on colored paper, label them, and arrange them around a large copy of this joke. "Knock, Knock!" "Who's there?" "People at our school . . . who REALLY care!"

New students will appreciate this bulletin board as they learn the names of important staff members who will help them.

Be on good terms with the custodian. He or she knows where things are, will help you with logistical concerns, will help provide clean-up materials and tools after a class party, and so on.

Colleagues

Foster good relationships with your colleagues by approaching every task and discussion with extreme professionalism. Treat all other staff members the way you would want to be treated.

Confidentiality in dealing with colleagues, students, or families is crucial. Relationships will grow stronger if other staff members learn that you can be trusted to share information with only those who need to know it.

Do your fair share. When committee assignments need filling or a faculty-sponsored event needs workers, volunteer.

Be responsible. If it is your week to clean the lounge or bring treats, be sure you complete these tasks or make arrangements for someone to take your place if you cannot perform that duty.

Come prepared. Staff meetings go more smoothly if everyone is focused and has the materials needed to make decisions. For collaborative planning with other teachers, have ideas and materials ready to share. This will endear you to those professionals.

Be prompt. If you have a duty, show up a minute early. If you have a meeting, be ready when it starts. If you have a report due, meet the deadline!

Recognize the accomplishments of others. When a colleague handles a discipline problem with expertise, comment. When the music teacher directs a great program, compliment. When the teacher next door puts up an exciting bulletin board, admire out loud. When the secretary helps you fill out a form, stick a note of appreciation on her computer!

Ask questions. Whether you are new to the school. the district, or the grade level, ask other staff members for advice. Everyone loves to feel like an expert, so give your colleagues a chance! Requesting advice and following it are two different things. If the suggestions you receive do not fit with your teaching methods, you are under no obligation to use them.

Be confident in your decisions. New teachers are sometimes inundated with too much advice from the veterans. Be courteous, tolerant, and appreciative, but follow your instincts about what will work for you.

Give yourself permission to try a technique, evaluate it, and revise it if it is not working for you. Trial and error is not a negative in the teaching world because teaching is not an exact science. There are multiple ways to do almost every task. So unless your administrator dictates a certain procedure, allow yourself the liberty to alter methods that are not immediately manageable for you.

Assistants

They have many different names, perform many important duties, and function at many different skill levels—they are Teaching Assistants, Paraprofessionals, or Aides. Whatever the name, the benefits of having them available to assist you are the same. They provide increased efficiency and effectiveness for you and your students. Treat them with respect. Treat them as professionals. Treat them as a vital part of your classroom and you will win their loyalty.

Give assistants clear, careful directions, written if possible. Confer with them early in the year to determine their proficiencies and preferences. Use that information to maximize their benefits to your classroom by applying their special skills and talents.

Outline your discipline policies, management systems, and procedures early in the year. Be thorough. Don't assume anything. Train them on copy machine, office procedures, and class rules. Familiarize them with the layout of your room and the location of supplies to minimize interruptions.

Encourage them to be self-starters and take initiative. Explain the importance of capitalizing on the "teachable moment" when it occurs. Insist on professionalism, confidentiality, and respect for students.

Establish a reporting system or periodic conference time.

Recognize and appreciate their efforts publicly.

VOLUNTEERS

Careful use of volunteers can make your work in the classroom more efficient and productive. Use the form on page 90 to learn about classroom volunteers, and communicate with them.

As you work together, you will discover the best way to work with them. Some will need a lot of direction, others will need little. Some will want to work with children, others will prefer to help you with paperwork. Some will be flexible, others will not. If you find that you really don't get along with a volunteer, be diplomatic about how you decline further services. Respond promptly to any offers to volunteer!

PROFESSIONAL ORGANIZATIONS

National Council of Teachers of Mathematics
1906 Association Drive
Reston VA 22091-1593

International Reading Association
800 Barksdale Road
P.O. Box 8139
Newark, DE 19714-8139
(1-800-336-7323)

National Council of Teachers of English
1111 Kenyon Road
Urbana IL 61801

National Council for the Social Studies
3501 Newark St., NW
Washington D.C. 20016

Smithsonian Institution
Office of Elementary Education
Arts and Industries Building
Washington, D.C. 20560

National Science Resources Center
National Academy Press
2101 Constitution Ave., NW
Washington, D.C. 20418

WONDERFUL WEB SITES FOR EDUCATORS

Busy Teachers' WebSite K–12
Provides lesson plans and activities in many categories for K-12 teachers.

http://www.ceismc.gatech.edu/busyt

Classroom Connect
Get ideas integrating the Internet into learning.

http://www.classroom.net

Discovery Channel School Online
A searchable database for K-12 teachers with lesson plans and links to other educational web sites.

http://www.school.discovery.com

Eduzone—"The Education Web Site"
Tips, handouts, trivia, scholarship and grant information, historical facts, and more are provided on this site.

http://www.eduzone.com

Education World®—Where Educators Go To Learn
Thousands of web sites that will interest educators are listed on this searchable site. Lesson plans, curriculum sources, and contemporary educational topics are included.

http://www.education-world.com

Brainstorm of the Day—Bright Ideas for Busy Teachers
This site offers ideas on classroom management, organization strategies, and mini-ideas that are linked to curriculum areas, includes ideas on using the Internet in your classroom.

http://www.teachnet.com

Library in the Sky
Over 6000 educational resources are offered on this site, including lesson plans, book suggestions, family support, and counseling help.

http://www.nwrel.org/sky/index.html

Kids Web: A World Wide Web Digital Library for Schoolkids
This easy-to-use site links students and teachers to informational topics, fun sites, and reference materials.

http://www.npac.syr.edu/textbook/kidsweb/indexold.html

OTHER TEACHING REFERENCES

The 7 Habits of Highly Effective People by Stephen R. Covey (Fireside, 1990). Learn characteristics to make your teaching more efficient, effective, and rewarding.

Skills for Success for Your Third Grader by Glenda Frasier (Frank Schaffer Pub., 1997) Suggestions to help you communicate programs and ideas to parents.

Summer Skills for the Third-Grade Graduate by Glenda Frasier (Frank Schaffer Pub., 1998) Ready-to-use reproducibles for students, thematically arranged and reinforcing many curriculum areas.

The First Days of School: How to Be an Effective Teacher by Harry K. Wong and Rosemary Tripi Wong (Harry K. Wong Publications, 1988). Sections for new and veteran teachers inspire and motivate.

Teaching and Learning in the Elementary School: Focus on Curriculum by Judy Reinhartz and Don M. Beach (Merrill-Prentice-Hall, 1997) An overview of curriculum areas with excellent resources and suggested activities.

> I never before understood the depth of gratitude a parent can feel for a teacher who creates a classroom environment that enables children to love learning, to exhibit genuine enthusiasm and excitement for purposeful and meaningful tasks, and to experience a feeling of belonging to a new community of friends.
>
> —Irene Hannigan

HOME/SCHOOL COMMUNICATION

Clear communication with the parent(s) or guardian(s) of each child is essential. Make your home/school connections frequent and concise. Because parents' schedules can be hectic, make it quick and easy for them to get the information they need. There are many ways to make a connection between home and school. The best way to do this is through communication. This can range from notes home to a monthly newsletter.

Parents may need multiple reminders for important events. Always date your written memos. Print your parent notes on bright-colored paper and always use the same color. Choose a color that demands attention, such as hot pink, for important communications to parents. Early in the year, alert parents that notes written on hot pink paper will be important notices from you!

Send home corrected work with comments so that the parents can see what their child is working on in class and how he or she is doing. Homework that requires adult contributions is another way to connect with the parents and help them be involved in the educational process.

Use the phone as a way to communicate any special concerns to the parent. Call at least one parent each week to compliment his or her child. The parents will love to hear good news from you, and they won't dread your calls.

Back-to-School Night

Back-to-School Night usually occurs within the first six weeks of school. Prepare in advance. This is your opportunity to let parents know what is going to happen in the upcoming academic year, to find out what questions they have, and how they can be involved in the instructional program. Make an information packet for parents that includes the following.

- Welcome letter
- Your background
- List of supplies that students need
- Class rules and consequences of breaking the rules
- School policy on absences and discipline
- Grading policies—yours and the school's
- Report card schedule and basis of your evaluations.
- Homework procedures and policies
- Field trip information
- A wish list—often parents want to provide materials that you can use with their children, such as disposable cameras, film processing, computer programs, materials for your centers or for special art projects, and specific books
- Any other information that you want parents to know or you think they might want to know

Keep the tone of the evening informal and comfortable. Review the packet with parents. Answer any questions that come up. Briefly talk about the curriculum that will be covered during the year. Display the curricular programs, including teacher's guides, your school has adopted and talk briefly about them. Give parents an opportunity to look over the materials. Many of the new math programs that emphasize thinking strategies rather than drill and memorization may be new to parents. You could even demonstrate a lesson and have the parents participate.

Parent/Teacher Conference

Parent/Teacher conferences usually occur midway into the second quarter of the school year. You meet personally with parents or caretakers of every one of your students to talk about the student's academic and social progress. Many teachers like to have the classroom filled with student work during conferences as it makes the students feel proud, and it gives parents an idea of what third-grade work looks like.

Generally the school or district has days set aside specifically for conferences, and specific guidelines about the minimal length of the conference. Frequently your in-class time with your students will be shorter on conference days. Usually you will be expected to put together the schedule of which parents you will see when. Some teachers like to assign times to parents without consulting the parents first, other teachers like to give parents the option to choose a "best time" and then juggle the schedule.

Your school may have specific notices you are required to send out. Others let you send whatever notice you want, as long as you send one out. Your school may provide you with a schedule of times to fill in with the names of parents who are coming, and when they are coming. Send reminder notices of the scheduled meeting the day before you are to meet. Include your school phone number.

> **Enthusiasm is contagious—and so is the lack of it.**
> —Anonymous

Post the schedule outside your door, and place a few chairs outside where parents can sit while they are waiting for you. Leave your door open so that the parents with whom you are talking will only stay for their allotted time. When they hear the next parents arrive, they will know that their time is almost up. Decide how inflexible you are going to be about your schedule. If a parent comes late, will you ask her or him to leave when the time is up, or will you run behind schedule a bit. Check with other teachers to see what they will be doing with late parents.

Prepare for your conference in advance. Outline the information you want to cover about each child so that when parents are there, you can remember all the important information. Group papers, portfolios, and files pertaining to each student and have them at hand when the parents walk through the door. You want to make the best use of the short time you have with the parents. Many schools and districts require you to turn in a sheet signed by the parents who have visited you. Ask them to sign this before you start the conference.

During the conference, put parents at ease by sharing a table. You may intimidate them if you sit at your desk while they are at a table or a child-sized desk. Always start with a positive remark about the student. Refer to your outline during the conference. Take notes of parent comments directly on your outline. File the outline as a benchmark against which to monitor the student's progress throughout the year. Provide the parents with a copy to take home with them if your school does not have a standardized form you are supposed to use.

Talk with parents during the conference, not at them. Remember, you are talking about their child. They know the child best, ask for their insights. Listen to the parents' concerns. Show them work samples and portfolio pieces to give them a picture of how their student is doing. They will be able to put the work in context if you have decorated the room with a variety of student work. Open the lines of communication. The parents, the student, and you are a team. The goal is for the student to succeed in school. Everyone wants the student to have a productive and enjoyable third-grade year.

Open House

Open House generally occurs within two months of the end of school. It is a showcase of the students' accomplishments during the school year. Display writer's workshop books, math projects, science discoveries, and other class projects.

The week before Open House have students create an invitation to the event which they take home to their parents.

Prepare for the visit by having each student prepare and decorate two folders from construction paper. One folder will store work that must stay in school and the other folder is for the parents to take home.

Have students design a tour of the classroom for their parents. Decide what centers they want to show their parents. Have students prepare a demonstration of a favorite group activity or show a video of in-class presentations.

Communications

At the end of every week send a calendar home with students for the next week. Include topics that will be studied, things the student needs to bring, and special events. The calendar can be set up as a template that can be quickly filled in and copied. Many computer software programs offer simple calendar templates.

Set up a class newsletter. Include columns such as "Things We Learned This Week," "Trash Treasures We Need," "Here's What's Coming Next," "Looking Ahead," and "Getting to Know . . . "(a short biography of a student, a teacher's assistant, or a school staff member). Writing and publishing it could be part of your technology curriculum.

At least once a month, send a letter home that addresses parenting issues. Magazines, professional journals, PTA groups, and educational organizations offer articles on topics like homework help, learning to read, helping children get along with each other, when to keep a sick child home, or ways to build a child's self-esteem. You might consider joining forces with other third-grade teachers to put this parenting magazine together.

Encourage Parental Involvement

Make your classroom an inviting place to visit.

Make parents feel welcome anytime.

Communicate about what is going on in class.

Avoid teacher-speak.

Teach them ways to help their children learn.

Clearly state your goals.

Affirm their roles as their children's first and most important teachers.

Involve them by requesting help or ideas.

At the beginning of the year, send home a copy of your class schedule. Invite parents to visit during times of special interest to them. Remind them to check in at the office upon their arrival. In some cases, you may want to ask that parents call or send a note to let you know they will be coming. You may also want to set parameters for visits, such as how long parents should stay based on how a particular student reacts when his or her parents are in the classroom.

Host a Family Night

Invite the whole family for an evening of math, art, or reading activities. Use your current thematic unit to tie this evening into the regular classroom. You could also turn the evening into a culminating activity for the thematic unit or a Writer's Workshop Portfolio Party.

Keep the evening short (an hour at most) and inexpensive. Use materials you have available at school. If space is limited, suggest only one member of the family come to each family night and then host more than one during the year. Involve students in every aspect of the plans.

HOMEWORK

In some schools and districts students begin receiving nightly homework in kindergarten. In others, third grade is the year when homework generally becomes an expected event each evening. A half-hour of homework is acceptable. A math worksheet, a spelling activity, or a social studies review would be appropriate homework for a third-grade student. Some students in third grade will be excited about researching and presenting reports. Most students are ready to acquire organization skills that will help them be more independent and guide them to accept responsibility for themselves.

Busy parents appreciate a management system that quickly lets them know what homework needs to be accomplished that day. Explain the process and the products you expect regarding homework at your Open House or Parent Meeting, or send a note home the first week of school explaining your requirements and expectations in a friendly manner. Use the homework assignment sheet to organize homework on a weekly basis (page 91). Avoid using teaching jargon in your communications with parents.

Give each student a homework folder. Colorful binders with interior pockets are ideal—inexpensive and durable. Each Monday evening, send the homework folder home with the weekly assignment sheet. You can request that specific homework be turned in on specific days, or that it all come in by Friday. If a student doesn't turn homework in on a regular basis, let the parents know, but emphasize that homework is the responsibility of the student.

For families who struggle with this process, schedule a conference that includes the child. Review the process with the student and his or her parents. It may be helpful to suggest that parents sign homework tasks before the child returns them to school until the student is ready to assume responsibility for his or her own homework.

CHAPTER FIVE: CLOSING THOUGHTS

ENGLISH LANGUAGE DEVELOPMENT

You may have students in your class who do not speak English as a first language. In schools where there are many students who speak languages other than English as a first language, you will probably have access to an English Language Development program with guidelines for its use outlined by your school or district. Remember learning a language is a process. It took you years to speak English well, and you may have been able to concentrate most of your language development on one language.

If you find yourself with a small group of non-English speaking students in your class, and you have no administrative support, check your school's resource room, local university library, or Internet resources for some specific plans and courses of study to assist the students. Some quick guidelines include providing picture cues for certain activities. Teach students the names of activities and materials (in the context of doing the activity) so that when they hear or see those words they will know what books or materials they need.

Assign the students peer mentors who can help them learn classroom vocabulary. When you change activities, take a moment to approach your non-English speaking students, look at them, and speak at a slower rate using a simple language structure with instructions. Model appropriate responses to questions.

87

Your non-English speaking students also come from cultures where acceptable body language differs from what you may be used to. Perhaps as a child you were raised to look at an adult when the adult was talking to you. Looking away was disrespectful. Many cultures consider a child who looks an adult in the face insolent and defiant, so a well-mannered child will never look at an adult directly. Increase your level of awareness of the body language of these students.

Include the students in activities. Model respect for their culture and their intelligence to the class. Set the tone for acceptance of these students in your class. Your students will follow you. What to you may be little acts of kindness may shine out as beacons of goodwill and inspiration to the student struggling to understand a new language and a new culture.

MAINSTREAMING

Mainstreaming means placing a student with disabilities in a regular education classroom. **IEP** means the *Individualized Education Program* required for each student receiving special education.

If you are the teacher of a student on an IEP, you are responsible for implementing the curriculum to fulfill the goals and objectives. The IEP team meets annually to discuss goals and objectives and to make sure that progress is being made.

However, you are not in this alone. Members of the IEP team should work closely with you. Help is available if you ask. Team members include the school nurse, the special education teacher, the school psychologist, a behavioral consultant, an occupational therapist, a special education supervisor, and other school personnel.

Students with special needs can be successful in the regular education classroom. Be receptive to and accommodate their individual needs.

COMMUNITY RESOURCES

If you are new to the community where you will be teaching, explore to discover resources that might heighten the effectiveness of your teaching. If you have lived in the community, but are new to teaching third grade, review the resources available that relate to your new curriculum. Visit the local visitors' bureau for sights of special interest and community service groups. Get a map of the state and learn the names of surrounding towns, counties, recreational areas, and regional sites. Check the yellow pages for businesses that correlate with units you will teach. Call the Chamber of Commerce, City Hall, or the County Courthouse and inquire about businesses that offer free items for education or field studies. Read the local newspaper for entertainment or cultural events. Become familiar with the diversity and cultures represented in your community. And finally, ask colleagues what resources they use or recommend for your grade level.

FIELD TRIPS

Many schools and districts have budgets dedicated to field trips that may be used to go to places designated by the school or district. The budgets may include use of a school bus and entry fees to designated destinations. In these cases you may be limited to a certain number of field trips per year and have other requirements you need to meet. Other schools and districts will give you more latitude in where and how frequently your class can travel. Check with your school early in the year to find out what your guidelines and requirements are. Frequently at schools and districts where the budget for field trips is limited, there are few restrictions in walking field trips that cost no money. If your school is in an area safe to walk, look for potential field trip destinations locally. Work them into your plans with appropriate preparation and follow-up activities.

WHEN YOU ARE ABSENT

Even if you enjoyed perfect health before you started working as a teacher, you will get sick. You are exposed to lots of germs in a school. Usually by your third year of teaching your immunity is built enough so that you don't catch every cold or other virus that comes through your classroom door. In addition, in-service educational experiences may be scheduled during the school day so that you must be away from your classroom.

Your school or district may have a service that arranges for substitutes or you may have to find your own. At the beginning of the year, find out what you need to do by asking another teacher or the school secretary. If you are able, leave plans for the substitute teacher. Use the form on page 92 to communicate with your "sub."

CHILD ABUSE

In many states teachers are required by law to report any suspicion of child abuse. Proving abuse is not your responsibility, but reporting suspicions of abuse is. Some schools will follow up a teacher's suspicions, other schools require the teacher to act alone. Check with your school or district about your legal responsibilities.

CLOSING WORDS

Teaching can be exhilarating and exhausting. Take care of yourself. Eat right, exercise regularly, and get enough rest. Pursue your hobbies and continue your personal development hand-in-hand with your professional development. Keep your life in balance, and you will be the most effective teacher you can be. I hope you have an exciting career.

Every second we live is a new and unique moment of the universe, a moment that never was before and never will be again. And what do we teach our children in school? We teach them that 2 and 2 makes 4 and that Paris is the capital of France. When will we also teach them what they are? We should say to each of them: Do you know what you are? You are a marvel. You are unique. In all the world there is no other child exactly like you. In the millions of years that have passed there has never been a child like you. And look at your body what a wonder it is! Your legs, your arms, your cunning fingers, the way you move! You may become a Shakespeare, a Michelangelo, a Beethoven. You have the capacity for anything. Yes, you are a marvel. And when you grow up can you then harm another who is, like you, a marvel? You must cherish one another. You must work—we must all work—to make this world worthy of its children.

—Pablo Casals

Volunteer Information Form

Name _____ Telephone Number _____

Yes! I'd love to volunteer to help at school!

Here are some ways I think I could help you!

☐ Read to students   ☐ Check papers

☐ Help students complete work   ☐ Organize the classroom library

☐ Put up bulletin boards   ☐ Supervise art/craft projects

☐ Cut out materials   ☐ Prepare snacks with children

☐ Play games with groups of students   ☐ Operate audio-visual equipment

☐ Supervise computer projects   ☐ Other: _____

☐ Listen to students read   _____

☐ Word processing/Electronic publishing   _____

Hobbies, collections, or special interests I have: _____

_____

_____

_____

The best time(s) for me to come: _____ _____

                                          (Day)   (Time)

- -

Date:

Hello _____ !

Thanks for helping today!

Here's what needs to be done!

_____   Date Needed _____

_____   Date Needed _____

_____   Date Needed _____

_____   Date Needed _____

_____   Date Needed _____

_____
Teacher's Name

Teacher: Photocopy the different halves of this form as you need them. See page 81 on volunteers.

Homework Assignments

Week of _____

Monday   Date: _____

_____

_____

Tuesday   Date: _____

_____

_____

Wednesday   Date: _____

_____

_____

Thursday   Date: _____

_____

_____

Friday   Date: _____

_____

_____

Long Term Projects: _____

_____

_____

Read 20 minutes every night.

Parent comments or questions: _____

_____

_____

SUBSTITUTE INFORMATION

Thanks for taking over!

Name tags are located _____

Seating chart is located _____

Class roster is located _____

For accurate information ask

_____

(staff member's name)

_____

(reliable student's name)

Lesson plans are located _____

Safety drill information is located _____

Teacher's guides are located _____

Today's schedule is located _____

Supplies you'll need today are located _____

Activities that MUST be accomplished today are_____

_____

If you have extra time, you could _____

_____

Special Notes _____

_____

_____

On the back of this sheet, please write a note about how the day went!

Teacher: Fill out the items that never change. Make a few copies and then just fill in the new information when you have to be absent. Keep some at home in case you are ill and may need to call in the information or send a copy with a colleague.

FS122005 Getting Ready to Teach Third Grade

STUDENT RECORD SHEET

News about

_____

(Write your name here!)

(Attach your photo here!)

What interesting place have you visited? _____

What is your favorite music group? _____

Do you have any collections or hobbies? _____

What outdoor sport do you like best? _____

What special skill would you like to learn? _____

What makes you feel important? _____

What is your favorite book? _____

What kind of book would you like to read next? _____

What do you worry about? _____

What is a new idea you heard or read about lately? _____

_____

What is your favorite thing to do with your family? _____

_____

Teacher: Have your students fill in this form at the beginning of the year. File it in their portfolios. At the end of the year have students do it again and compare their responses. You can file record sheets in permanent portfolios, or make copies for the portfolios and return the originals to students at the end of the year.

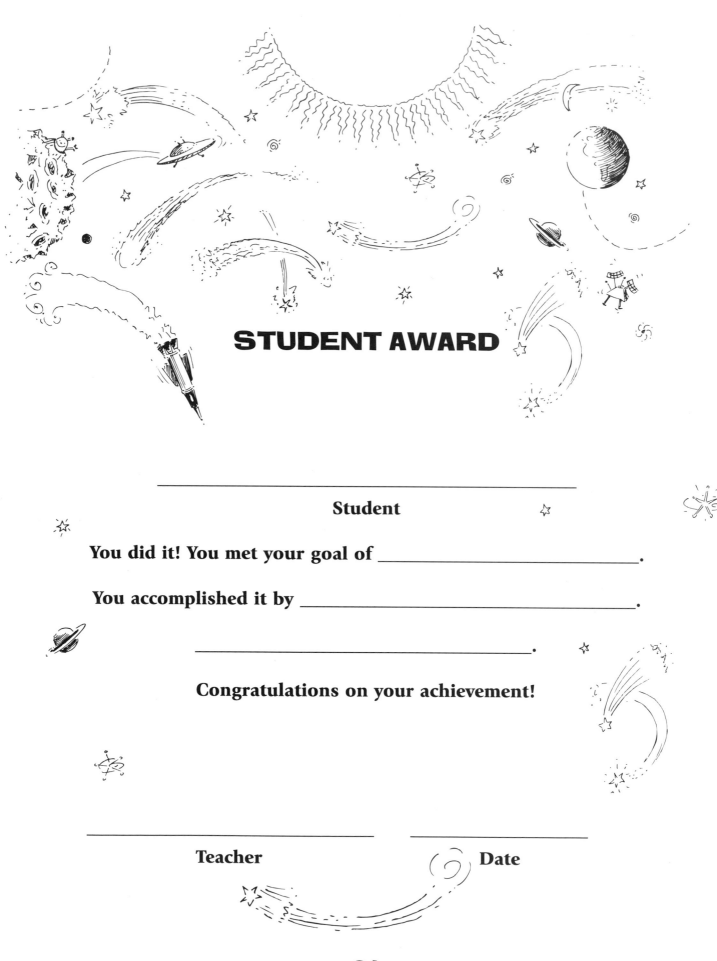

STUDENT AWARD

_____

Student

You did it! You met your goal of _____.

You accomplished it by _____.

_____.

Congratulations on your achievement!

_____   _____

Teacher   **Date**